IF I HAD $1,500
I WOULD CLEAN
MY KARMA

IF I HAD $1,500 I WOULD CLEAN MY KARMA

Ada Garwood

To order additional copies of this book, contact:
Xlibris Corporation
1-888-795-4274
www.Xlibris.com
Orders@Xlibris.com
118974

Contents

Dedication

To my husband, my sons, my parents and my many friends who made life possible during an impossible time. Thanks to Dr. Olga J., Gladys O., Selma B., Natalie, Sara A., Ben, Mike G., Judge Freida H. and Dr. Fritz.

Chapter 1

DEAR YOUNG PERSON: DO NOT
ABANDON YOUR DREAMS

Ever since I was old enough to hold a pen in my hand and to write, at about eight years of age, I wanted to become a writer. When I grew up I became a writer and was published, but my jealous husband tried to stop me from continuing to write. He beat me and my children and I knew we had to escape him and live our own lives away from him.

The children and I escaped and I realized that I had saved myself and them, but had abandoned my own true self as an author. Even though I worked as a writer to earn a living, I worked as a writer for hire which meant I wrote only things other people assigned me to write that were not necessarily relevant to my inner feelings as an author. Many non-fiction themes appealed to me and I enjoyed tackling those. But I wanted to write fiction and the stress of my life and the need to earn a living stopped me just as it had my own father.

Dear young person:
If you have a dream for your life, do not abandon yourself as you encounter rough times the way that I did.

We lived in many places when I was a child. We went from our apartment in the Bronx with a grand piano and botanical gardens outside the window to living in one room with a bathroom down the hall shared with other roomers. I had no room of my own. Then we moved into my grandmother's apartment and we lived with my grandparents and all their children and grandchildren who lived nearby or in her apartment. I was seven and I began pretending I was an actress speaking on the radio. I would mouth the words of the radio voices I heard, and pretend I was one of them.

I was surrounded by a lot of unsophisticated, poor, struggling people. These were critical years. When I was eight, my thirteen-year-old cousin babysat me so my mother could play cards with her friends. But then, she never wanted to be bothered with me anyway. I wrote my first book at eight. I lived inside the books I read. My brother was born when I was eight and one-half and from then on my mother was occupied with her new baby and was happy to abandon me.

I was very alone and had no relationship with her that I can remember—but I was very successful in school and had many friends. I didn't hang around her too much. I played out huge, dramatic stories with my friends. She left us alone due to her sense of importance—that was a blessing. Somewhere about the age of twelve, I got my period—she slapped me across my face.

When I was thirteen, I met a twenty-year-old man just returned from the navy. He waited for me to grow up. When I reached eighteen, five years later, he had become a millionaire. He asked my parents' permission to ask me to marry him. Then he asked me. I refused. I was too young. I was planning to work my way through college because I had recently been given a scholarship.

Going back a bit, after my sweet sixteen party, held in a basement in my neighborhood in Brooklyn, I went to the University of Wisconsin—1500 miles from home. At sixteen I was on my own with five hundred dollars from my father's insurance policy to pay for four years of college. My mother went to work to help me pay expenses. I went to work at the college to make some money, as well. I also worked hard at my studies to try out for a scholarship. I went to Wisconsin because I was a journalism major. I wanted to be a writer. In high school I had been editor-in-chief of the high school newspaper and we all visited Columbia University to receive a prize. Our school newspaper had won the prize that year as the best high school newspaper in the country.

At the University of Wisconsin I told my English teacher that I wanted to become a writer. He shocked me when he said that I was already a writer. Ever since I was eight, I used to write poetry and stories and often recited my work to groups of people. In the summers, around the campfire, I read my poetry to about fifty families. At sixth grade graduation, I read before all the parents, grandparents and children, about five hundred of them.

In sixth grade, my teacher, Mrs. Gordon asked to adopt me; she had had no children of her own. She wrote me a letter when I graduated from sixth grade telling me that my future had great potential.

For some reason I grew up thinking that I needed to carry the ills of the world on my back. From eight years to fourteen I read every book I could get at the Grand Army Plaza Library. I even was old enough at eleven to take the subway to the library and bring books home. At twelve years of age, I got a job at the summer resort hotel as a counselor taking care of the little kids in day camp. After all, I had been babysitting for money since I was eight years old.

At sixteen I went to Wisconsin. It was strange because then I found out I was Jewish. I started living on this enormous campus in Madison, Wisconsin. It had lots of lakes. I got a job working for the widow of the local newspaper editor of the Journal. I fed her two children lunch every day when they came home from school. I had to walk two miles each way to feed them lunch and then get back to classes. They were nice little boys.

At the dorm I lived in I was the only Jewish girl from New York. I visited the Unitarian church with a friend and met a boy named Wesley. He was Jewish. He wrote sonnets to me and took me on my first date for my seventeenth birthday on February 25th. We went to dinner and dancing and I felt like I was living in a fairy tale. That date, February 25, was also the first time Sylvia Plath met Ted Hughes at Cambridge University, a few years later.

Wesley wanted me to visit his parents. I did not understand then that he wanted to marry me. During Christmas vacation from school I went to visit my friend Marian in Chicago. Her parents wanted to give me a scholarship in honor of her stepbrother who had died in World War II. She had been a janitor's child and this wealthy lawyer and his wife had adopted her. She had three other brothers and sisters that were adopted by other families after her mother died. This family raised her and she studied ballet and was accepted into the Chicago Ballet. That summer, at seventeen, she got polio and could never dance again. She ended up at the University of Wisconsin in our beginning English class.

We became good friends—and she wanted me to receive the scholarship in honor of her stepbrother. Wesley wanted me to transfer to the University of Chicago because he thought I would learn faster and graduate more quickly. He had gone there at fourteen and graduated at seventeen and was in Law School at eighteen. They wouldn't let him into law school at seventeen, so he had to spend a year taking courses in

Milwaukee where he lived. He studied Japanese and anthropology.

I met with the person at the University of Chicago who administered the Gulbens Scholarship but I had no idea what he thought. After Christmas vacation, I went back to school. I went to visit the person at the University of Wisconsin to find out about the scholarship. He blurted out that Wesley was getting counseling because he wanted to marry me. I was very upset. I didn't want to get married young. I wanted to finish college and write. It was upsetting. I had also made friends with the editor of the university school newspaper and he told me he was on a Congressional scholarship. He was allowed to nominate the successor to his scholarship. He told me that he would nominate me. The scholarship would pay my tuition for the rest of my college years. So, now I was up for two scholarships.

I had gotten an A+ in my journalism course and the head of the department wanted to see me. I visited with him and he, too, said I already could write like a journalist. He suggested I major in history and other subjects and become a content expert.

Meanwhile my roommate had declared me weird because I wrote poetry and my beau sent me sonnets. She sent me to the psychologists at the university when I got upset and they gave me ink blot tests. I did this, and when I got to the hospital where the psychologists were they told me to take off my clothes and get in a bed.

I told them there were still classes I needed to attend. They said I couldn't go back to school. I had to stay in the hospital. They took me in a wheelchair to Wisconsin Neuropsychiatric and there an attendant put electrodes on my head. I was scared to death. After this visit, I went back to the room I shared with the daughter of a farmer who had just had an eye operation and whose eyes were bandaged. I had been in the infirmary only once before for a cold I had, a few months back.

The psychologists questioned me now about my job and why I needed to earn money. They wanted to know why I walked four miles a day in the dead of winter—and couldn't I have found a better way to earn money. I didn't know that later they would say this was a sign of instability.

My zoology teacher was the only adult I knew from New York. She was a nice lady named Molly. I had met her on the train coming from New York. She kind of adopted me. Molly called my mother when all this happened. My mother got a letter from the university saying I had to drop out of school. She got in touch with them and said she was coming out. She told them there was nothing wrong with me. She was right.

But now they proceeded to fill me with truth serum. Wesley sent me sonnets at the hospital, but they wouldn't let him visit. Anyway, it didn't matter. I was like a broken thing. I said good-bye to all my friends. The college editor told me I had his scholarship—but I couldn't use it. I had to go home with my mother to an uncertain future. The doctor on duty when she arrived told her to get me out of there. He agreed with my mother that nothing was wrong with me. I was just a little over seventeen years old when I returned on the train with her to New York.

My cousin was a pediatrician and I was sent to live with her because she was a doctor. When I came to stay with her and her husband, who was a surgeon, they had a little three-year-old daughter with curly blonde hair who loved to dance. The pediatrician's sister was an attorney and she came to visit. She asked me what happened. I told her. She said she didn't see anything abnormal in my behavior; I was acting like any seventeen-year-old would have acted. She asked me to visit a client of hers whom she represented as his attorney on a book he was writing. I went with my mother up to Park Avenue to meet this tall, Viennese psychiatrist. He talked with me and said he didn't see anything wrong, either. He had a psychologist administer Rorschach tests and said they were fine.

Dr. Fritz helped me go back to college because I wanted to study and he helped me to get a scholarship to Bennington College and, of course, he had to vouch for my sanity. By now, these lunkheads in Wisconsin had practically destroyed my future. But I kept on going at Bennington until I graduated as a literature major, got a job on a magazine and after graduation wrote my first novel, *Suns of Darkness*.

Chapter 2

EARLY YEARS: BEFORE THE MARRIAGE

I always felt cut off from the world I had grown up in and I wandered about a lot. I couldn't bear the listless tenements and the people without hope. I had to leave. My loneliness among these people was unbearable, so I moved into a basement apartment and sculpted clay figures which brought some relief.

Wanting to be an artist like my father had never let himself become, I was angry at him for brooding all the time and never producing his art. I decided that I would produce art and nothing or no one would stop me in the way my father allowed himself to be stopped. My father said he didn't produce art because he had to earn a living for his family, but I felt he was using that as an excuse. I didn't really know what kept him from giving his art to others.

At times, I thought it might be some basic stinginess about giving, but then I observed him torturing himself when he couldn't paint. I identified with his struggle to be an artist. Sometimes I thought maybe my mother held him back, then at other times I blamed him. It always angered me because I could not understand an artist not wanting to let go of their art and not giving it to the world, and then brooding because it was still inside them.

This seemed like a paradox to me.

My father said he worked hard every day and didn't have the time—he had a family to support. Inside himself, he always sustained his dream. I shared that dream with him, but I wouldn't give it up for anyone. My parents got tangled up in my dreams of becoming an artist. My mother complained:

"Why doesn't he do something—instead of brooding. Either you do it—or you don't."

Inside myself, I sympathized with my father. The more my mother chided him, the more I felt for his plight. As I tried to untangle my art from my parents' vantage points, I felt a strange kind of restlessness. I knew that most women were expected to settle down in houses with thickly padded carpets weighed down by hundreds of pounds of furniture, draperies, chandeliers and cupboards filled with silver and china. This was definitely not for me because I wanted only one thing—to be an artist.

There were wrought-iron bars on the windows outside my dark, basement apartment. Alone much of the time, I was learning to sculpt. I also painted wild, colorful paintings. Inside myself I recognized how terribly frightened I was, but I could not run from my inner fears because they were always with me, they always followed me, and anyway, I didn't understand them.

Isolation didn't bother me because I felt I was on the path toward something I really wanted. I didn't want to brood in frustration like my father, so I painted wild and colorful paintings. People were startled at the freedom of expression in my paintings, even though inside myself I was terribly frightened and did not feel free at all.

I just kept on working at my art. Trying to work in all the different media that I could: Japanese brush painting, oils, clay carvings, enamel and dripping on masonite boards with cans of paint like Jackson Pollack. My work carried me along like waves in the ocean and it all came so easily to me. I even inspired my father to begin to paint again.

He began painting the rabbis he had seen as a child in somber grays and blacks. He painted seascapes, and his waves were delicate with white lace sea foam. When he painted a wine glass in still life, you could almost feel the glass come off the canvas.

I thought my father's work showed great promise. I watched him emerge as an artist at the age of fifty. But I didn't want to wait until fifty to emerge. I wanted to be an artist—here and now, at age nineteen.

Chapter 3

IVY LEAGUE WOMEN'S COLLEGE

It is miraculous that I sat on a bus going through New England. I sat there wearing a navy blue dress with matching bag, shoes and hat. The dress had touches of white lace around the collar and I wore white gloves. I was on my way to an interview at an Ivy League women's college. I even looked as if I belonged there.

My first interview had been in New York City and after sending in my application I had been invited to come and visit the school. When I got off the bus I was met by the Director of Admissions and she took me to the campus in her car. I saw a series of small cottages lining a central common. This school in Vermont was light years away from the slum I had grown up in. Girls sure of their ivy league status strolled around the campus on the paved paths on both sides of the green. With the director I visited the dorms, the library and the classrooms and I was overwhelmed.

The dreams I had had of learning and the chance to study now seemed possible. I didn't have to live in the slums forever. I was nervous as I watched the lucky girls who were strolling in and out of the classrooms chatting and laughing, and appearing to be very comfortable with themselves.

As I sat in the Admissions Office, the dean extended her hand towards me. I looked out the large picture window behind her desk. "How are you?" she asked.

I shook her hand and said, "Fine."

We talked for a while and suddenly she looked at me and asked, "Why do you look so frightened?"

I was surprised. "I'm just afraid," I answered.

"Not of us—really, nobody has to be afraid at our school," she said and smiled.

I smiled and tried to believe her.

When the interview was over I sat there almost in a trance, for my dreams might come true. Right there, the dream of a fine woman's college offering to pay my way on a scholarship was happening to me. I felt dizzy from shock.

This was an incredible dream coming true for me, a girl who used to spend her time on tar-covered rooftops looking out over the dusty city tenements trying to find stars in the sky at night.

When the interview was over, the dean got up and said, "Good-bye for now," and we shook hands.

I barely heard what she said during the interview. I answered her anyway. In truth, I had never seen such a place as this. It looked so beautiful, with grass and trees and lovely brick walks. There were tall trees at the back of the college and it reminded me of the forests I used to walk in as a child when we went to the summer place we rented.

As we walked to the station wagon that would take me back to the bus stop, I saw girls sitting out under a tree with their professor. They were reading poetry aloud. Where I came from, most of the people who lived in the tenements had never read a poem in their lives except for the ones they got on greeting cards. Here, everyone took these things for granted. I couldn't believe it.

I took the next bus back to New York City.

As we passed large houses and trees I realized I was going to escape the slums I had grown up in and at last I could be free.

In a few days I received a letter informing me that I had been awarded a scholarship. I had escaped. I was going to be free to be myself and do the things I loved.

Chapter 4

CHILDREN BORN TO POVERTY

No one who has not experienced poverty can understand it. Children who have never known this are not going to understand. Unfortunately, poverty turns the young against the world at an early age. To hear the bitterness and frustration in a child's heart requires a very good ear. Few of us have it.

The sense that there is nothing you can have creeps into the bones of the children of the poor. They are taught their lessons at a very young age. They develop defensiveness, lower their aspirations and their self-esteem. The world will not work until the children of the poor are taught to want and to hope and to expect like other children. Every step along the way for these children is hampered by the difficulty of an environment that yields little hope. When pitted against children of affluence, they cannot win. There are a few exceptions.

It is always the exceptions that make the poor dream that a way out is possible. A family earning just a pittance, fathers eking out their existence as clerks or waiters, mothers at home as housewives surrounded by furniture bought with wedding present money . . . The glimmers of hope for me when I was growing up were the people who believed in beauty and searched for it.

The library was filled with magnificent words, and miles and miles of books. The museums had beauty and the botanical gardens outside my window freed me from the dingy tenement that I lived in. As I looked out the window at the flowers, I dreamed and knew my mother didn't want me to live her life of agony and poverty. She dreamed of education as a way out of this trap.

So I read my books and burned with examples of the exceptions. I tried to follow in their footsteps and finally one day I arrived at an upscale New England girl's college on a crisp autumn day when the trees were bursting with magenta and bright orange leaves. I had received a scholarship to attend this college. I stood on the campus holding my breath at the beauty I beheld. At last I had escaped.

I remembered back to the early years of my adolescence when I rode buses through suburbia and saw beautiful mansions with large green lawns, and I believed that those children had the best of all possible worlds. It was a mistake.

Only when I arrived at the New England girl's school did I learn what really went on inside these houses, what misery these people brought upon themselves. The girls told me about their families, and my pictures of peace and tranquility were replaced with Gothic horror tales. One girl's family consisted of her mother and father and her mother's lover, unbeknownst to her father as her lover, but only as a boarder with the family. Another girl talked about her Westchester mansion where her mother was housed with day and night nurses to keep her from repeated suicide attempts.

I pondered these things, trying to understand. The very amount of money used to care for the lawns of some of these places would have supported my whole family. Here were women with every opportunity, at least on the surface, going berserk in so many ways. It made me wonder about life. There were so many people I had known with so little, and now for the first time, I saw people squandering what they had with little respect or understanding for what they were doing.

What happened in those fashionable beach houses so rustic and weathered along the shore of Fire Island or the beaches at the Hamptons or on the Connecticut shore that insured that the path of their young people so closely resembled the path of their parents?

I look back to the days when I walked the bleak streets of Brooklyn, looking at the slums and the faces of the poor. I wonder what fires fed their spirit in the dismal, dark holes they called home. What fires built sparks in their hearts that made them dare to paint or sing or write, against all odds?

Perhaps it was a blind belief in this spark that made a small boy carry his violin for blocks and blocks to take his lesson. Or for another, who sat relentlessly sketching and sketching and one day a dream came true when he was accepted in art school.

Many young people wanted to leave the ghetto and the darkness of its despair and poverty. They searched in the public library, at every museum, scrounged every pencil and piece of paper they could find to write their poetry or draw their sketches. They worked days and studied nights, still believing that they could capture their dreams one day.

I decided that life was not a question of justice, but one of possibility. I wondered about life then, feeling shocked at the darker recesses of the human heart. I wondered bitterly why people wasted so much of their precious humanity and, certainly, their opportunities.

Chapter 5

MY COLLEGE ADVISOR, KENNETH BURKE:
A KIND, UNDERSTANDING FRIEND

Many years ago, in the 1950s, I met Ralph Ellison—the author of *The Invisible Man*. He was visiting Shirley Jackson and Stanley Edgar Hyman at Bennington College. Stanley Edgar Hyman was my advisor and I was studying writing at the college. My major was literature.

I was in my last two years at college there. Stanley Edgar told me Ralph Ellison was staying with them and Shirley was baking him brownies. He had hit a writer's slump and he was their house guest working up there on his next book. *The Invisible Man* had been a huge success and he was trying to do a new book. They were friends and supported his efforts on his new book.

I never thought I would look back to those days and would write a book myself called *The Invisible Woman*. If I don't call it that, it is still the story of my life which is totally invisible. Who I appear to be is a total fiction—and who I am in truth is invisible. My real persona is missing inside the fiction I present to everyone.

As the years have moved on the fiction itself has more and more become what the world thinks I truly am. This, of course, feels like a heavy, overweight costume that hides the truth. This is a mask worn over the self to pretend like a kabuki player that I am not who I really am—but rather the face that I present to others.

At my weekly meetings with S. E. Hyman we would discuss my choice for a thesis. When we were accepted in the upper section of the college we were expected to develop a thesis on a subject agreed upon by a committee of the faculty and my advisor. The year before I had worked with Kenneth Burke who used to commute to Bennington every other week and every other year from New Jersey. I was delighted to study with him; his method of literary criticism was something I really enjoyed doing. It was called indexing. I had talked with him the year before about writing a novel as my thesis—doing a creative work for graduation.

He was a short, little man who looked a lot like my own father with his grey mustache and graying hair. As my advisor the year before he requested the creative thesis be approved for graduation, but he told me it was turned down. "They want you to write a critical thesis. The faculty committee does not want creative writing as a fulfillment of your degree."

I was twenty years old then, I had already struggled since the age of eight to become a creative writer and I asked, "Why?" I was upset. "You see, I've been here on a scholarship and I've had to work my way through Bennington babysitting for Howard Nemerov and S. E. Hyman and Shirley Jackson, by waiting on tables for my meals, and by working as secretary to the Dean of Students for money to buy books and pens. When I leave Bennington College, I will have to work full time—as I do now when I get time off in the summer and the winter terms. The money I earn at these jobs pays for my room and board. Luckily, the scholarship pays my tuition. I know I will have to support myself. This is my only chance to have the time to write a novel. I want to use this time."

Kenneth Burke looked at me. "They won't give you your degree for a creative thesis, only for a critical thesis on an author you select."

I was shaken by this decision because none of those faculty members understood my life. They decided. Since I would not get my college degree if I bucked their system, I acquiesced.

"O.K.", I answered with a sad feeling. "I'll do a critique of Dostoevsky's *The Idiot.*"

Kenneth Burke replied, "That should satisfy them."

"I'll use your indexing technique for the analysis," I said.

He smiled. "You know writers go *through* college, not *to* college."

He continued, "Many years ago, I woke up one Sunday morning to see the front page headline of the New York Times Book Review read, "KENNETH BURKE IS DEAD!"

"The reviewers meant it," and they were going to bury my work as quickly as they could. It was about my creative writing—a novel I had written. They panned me devastatingly. So badly, I had to redo my entire life. After being a creative writer, I turned to teaching and criticism. And these books, *Rhetoric of Motives* and *Grammar of Motives*, are still in print. But, my novels, short stories and poems have never been published since that day."

I didn't really understand the depth of Kenneth Burke's statements at the time. I was on fire. I was going to be a writer—no matter what, I thought.

Even if they forced me to do this critical thesis, I would learn more about writing as I did it and when I got out of Bennington College, and was on my own, I would write a novel. And so for now—it would be a critique of *The Idiot*.

Kenneth Burke understood how badly I felt. He tried to be comforting. "It will be alright," he said gently as I left my counseling session with him.

I walked down the sloping green hill back to my dorm which lay at the bottom of the walk and which I had renamed *Ward # 6*, rather than Franklin House, as it was officially known.

Update: I recently looked up Kenneth Burke in my Encyclopedia of Literature and found that he had died in 1994 at the age of 96. I asked myself why I had not gone to see him in all those years. He had been a kind and understanding friend.

Chapter 6

SYLVIA PLATH WANTED TO MEET
SHIRLEY JACKSON, BUT DIDN'T

The "best laid plans" is what I am thinking now. How easy it was for me to move away from my burning desire to write and publish. I think a lot these days about Sylvia Plath who was my contemporary. She was at Smith and I was at Bennington. That's where the comparison ends.

She went to *Mademoiselle* Magazine for the guest writer summer college girl stint. So did the girl whose father owned a string of hardware stores in Brooklyn, New York. I met the hardware heiress when I went to Fire Island after I graduated from Bennington College. It was the July 4th weekend and I came to visit Adana's family's summer house on Fire Island. I came surrounded with protection. My mother trudged along in the sand with us as did my friend, Jared B. who had just returned from Panama and a stint in the army that left him devastated. I had met Jared when I was camp counselor at fourteen years of age and for some reason he fell in love with me thinking I was like his former girlfriend Becky.

He, too, worked at summer camp and the counselors in the male dorm, all guys from Ivy League and some not so Ivy League colleges told me he had a crush on me. They were all in their early twenties and I was still a little kid, although no one noticed that.

One divorced mother wanted to leave her six-year-old daughter with me and go back to her job and her divorce in the city.

"You can have a room in the hotel and live with my little girl," she pleaded. "She loves you."

I loved the little girl, too—but I was still a kid myself. I couldn't take responsibility for this woman's child for the entire summer while she tried to figure her life out.

I said, "no."

I remember this woman; she looked like a filly and wore a braid or pony tail on the back of her head. I did like the little girl, but I didn't want to take over raising her child, even for the summer.

Getting back to Jared B. By some chance I wandered into the boys' dorms one day, and several of them said, "Please, let us cut a lock of your hair and leave it on his pillow. The guy's got a massive crush on you . . ."

"No, guys . . ."

These Yale, Harvard and Columbia freshmen were ready to tease Jared B. into oblivion.

"No," I repeated.

Later I met Jared B.'s parents who asked me to dinner with his family at the hotel they were staying at. I went.

His mother talked to me privately and told me her son loved me and wouldn't I be nice to him—at least, as a friend.

So, I did become his friend and tried to see him in the winter when camp was over.

As time went on I went away to the University of Wisconsin and returned devastated by their psychiatry department who fed me "truth serum" and thought I was pregnant when I was still a virgin—all because the boy I dated wrote sonnets to me and I knew that I still wasn't ready for marriage . . . sonnets or not.

I was sixteen. Still a child. I had met my Seventh Day Adventist roommate on the street in Madison, Wisconsin when I first arrived and was looking for a place to stay. We started to chat and found ourselves in front of the same rooming house. There was one room left, so we decided to room together.

Belza was a graduate student in physical education from Salt Lake City, and I was a budding poet from Brooklyn, New York. I had never been away from home except to work at summer camp every year since I had been twelve. My mother and family boarded for the summer a few miles down the road from the camp near Lake Stonington where I had gone since I was three years old. So I knew the countryside in upstate New York, but I had never lived away from home. The trouble started when I began writing poetry and also was dating a writer of sonnets who left them under our door. In Belza's world, girls did not go out on dates with men nor did they hold hands or kiss them until after they were married.

She reported me to the school psychologists who called me in and gave me all kinds of psychological tests and also hauled me into the infirmary when I had a cold and scared me half to death. It was all very bewildering. But now, in the late 1950s, I was twenty plus years old, had graduated from Bennington College and was ready to write my first novel, or so I thought.

Anyway, to continue, Jared B. and I had remained quasi-buddies over the years, and I even would try to fix him up with girls he might like.

This July 4th weekend he had just returned from Panama (it must have been the Korean War); now he was out of the army and wanted to visit. I asked him to come along with my friend, Adana, my mother and myself to Adana's parents' summer house on Fire Island. He offered to drive all of us to Bayside, Long Island, this July 4th weekend and we boarded the ferry. It was my first time on the Fire Island Ferry. There were lots of New Yorkers on the boat, all looking sun tanned and chic in their beach attire, all ready for the opening summer weekend.

Jared was glad to get away. I did not have any interest in him as a beau, but I cared for him after so many years as a friend. I wanted him to be happy.

When we arrived at Ocean Beach Adana's mother and father were waiting at the dock with pre-purchased tickets for the ferry. Her father took our bags and deposited them in a little red wagon. Adana's father, Andrew, was wearing a beret, a white striped tee shirt, navy boxer swimming trunks and sneakers. Adana's mother was wearing washed denim Bermudas and a big straw sun hat with a denim shirt. They stood behind one of these metal chain-link school type fences at the gates to the dock. The metal fence was twelve feet tall. Andrew gave the attendants tickets for all of us and we were ransomed from behind the fence. His grey hair peeked out of the sides of his dark blue beret. He was balding under the beret, except for his grey sideburns.

My mother exited the ferry in her Brooklyn cotton house dress and her beige sandals. She was definitely not the usual Bennington College graduate's family member. She had gone to work in a factory at fourteen years old and was the child of a Polish immigrant barber. She had come to this country when she was twelve years old to escape the pogroms in Poland. She came with her five brothers and sisters and her parents from Warsaw.

She chatted with Adana's parents. We all trudged through the hot sand for almost a mile to the summer house which was four houses back from the ocean and three houses back from the bay. Many years later so many houses were washed out to sea by hurricanes that they became the second house from the ocean. They ultimately gave a sand dune in front of their house to Adana when she married Kevin and I understand they built a summer house there for themselves and their children. With the inroads of time and the weather it was eventually the first house at the ocean front.

Of course at this time, as we trudged through the sand, Adana was still in college and fairly overweight—a very tall girl of five feet eleven and quite a large young woman. I remembered first seeing her at college in a bright, orange felt jumper and she looked enormous. She made a grand, bright entrance when she arrived at the dorm.

I actually got to be her caretaker at Bennington when the college social worker asked if Adana could live near me at the dorm. Would I watch over her, as she put it, because she and another girl, Bee had terrorized a freshman girl and scared her to death. This girl, Bee was a junior and the dean asked her to leave, but Adana was a freshman and they didn't want to throw her out if she could be rehabilitated.

But now the school social worker asked me to look after her, just as at summer camp the divorced mother wanted me to watch her daughter. They moved her next door to me at the dorm I lived in, and that was part of the reason it was nicknamed *Ward # 6,* I believe after a Chekhov story by that name.

But here I was, now graduated and visiting Adana's beach house and trudging through the scorching, hot sand on a fiery, sunny July day to get to their getaway house on Fire Island.

When we all arrived we saw the place which had been built by Andrew, Adana's father. He told us that the original house had two rooms and that he had added on all the others. There were four rooms with windows that had beds built into them, also a wooden deck patio with a garden, and two sets of double—bedded rooms past the kitchen that sat out on another large wooden deck. An extra single-bedded room on the side of the original house looked out to the ocean.

Ocean breezes whipped through the salty air. I looked at the wild roses shooting up from the sandy garden. Adana's father was a New York trial attorney and her mother had been a publicist for the Museum of Modern Art and The New School for Social Research, both establishments founded by her friends. Adana's mother had been the first woman movie critic for a New England newspaper after she graduated from Radcliffe and a journalism school in New York. But, going back a bit, she had been a publicist for a movie conglomerate. Later Adana told me she had even taken a group of film students to Russia to meet Serge Eisenstein, the great Soviet movie director. That summer, when she went to Russia, she left her children with Andrew and the maid, Dora and their governess, an Irish nanny who made bacon sandwiches for Adana's brother Bentley. Adana's mother was a thoroughly modern woman.

Evangeline had attended a private preparatory Latin School and Radcliffe in the nineteen teens and twenties and her friends' names read like "Who's Who in America." She married Andrew later in the 1920s. He was a young lawyer who'd grown up in Brooklyn, son of a widowed mother and a rabbi father who had died young.

Andrew, Adana's father, had fought in World War I, and when he came back alive he was unable to finish college. So he went to work as an intern in a law firm where his cousin worked as a secretary. He ended up going to law school. He was a self-made man and a devoted father. When he married Evvie she was just out of journalism school. At her wedding she wore black as a Dadaist gesture, and Adana's brother, Bentley, was born seven months later in Boston.

Evvie's father was a doctor who came over from London and settled in Boston. He had three daughters in the early 1900s and was very disappointed because he wanted a son who would follow in his footsteps and become a doctor. He was delighted that his first grandchild was a boy and he took him to live with him in Boston. Evvie went back to New York to live on Madison Avenue with her new husband Andrew and left Adana's brother Bentley in Boston. Her father was delighted. He now had the future doctor in his hands. He was a man who founded two hospitals in Boston and was beloved by all his patients. Now he believed his dreams could come true. Sadly, he died sixteen years later while climbing four flights of stairs to visit a patient. At that time his grandson was a student at Harvard with the intention of becoming a doctor like his grandfather, just as his grandfather had always dreamed that he would.

Adana's mother and father had planted the light green lettuce-like plants surrounding the garden. The wooden deck stretched around the house and you could spray water on your sandy feet before coming inside. Out on the deck were some turquoise-colored canvas sling chairs from which you could get a commanding view of the sand dunes and the ocean.

I had never visited anyone who owned even one house before I went to Bennington College. Now I was visiting a family that had two. When we arrived, we found two guests were already there. That brings me back to the Sylvia Plath part of the story. There was a brunette, ponytailed girl who was *zaftig* and looked a lot like that divorcee who wanted me to babysit her daughter when I was fourteen. This girl (I don't remember her name—and it really doesn't matter) was playing house with Adana's brother.

Like Sylvia Plath she was a guest editor at *Mademoiselle*. She hoped to continue her studies at college and become an English professor one day. She went to Wellesley College.

Adana's brother was older than us by five years. He had graduated from Harvard and Columbia. He was now on his own as an entrepreneur and he appeared to be with her.

At any rate, the parents talked about why Adana had no dates.

I remember my mother talking to Adana's mother about this serious problem. I don't remember what advice she gave her—and it really doesn't matter now. Adana eventually married Kevin, a boy she knew from high school, and they celebrated their fiftieth wedding anniversary in 2009. When they were on their honeymoon in Cuba during the Christmas holidays, they heard shooting outside their hotel windows and that was the very week Castro took over Cuba. They had to catch the first plane out of there and they did.

I eventually married Adana's brother, the young man who was playing house with the guest *Mademoiselle* editor from Wellesley. She ended up dating Jared B for a while, since they both lived in Brooklyn. And, of course, Sylvia Plath married Ted Hughes and began her illustrious career as a poet and novelist before she committed suicide in 1963. Sylvia always wanted to meet Shirley Jackson. That wasn't really hard to do—I wish I had known when I was babysitting at Bennington for Shirley. It seemed strange that Sylvia never got over to Vermont to meet Shirley, since it wasn't really that far from Boston where she lived. At that time I was about to write my first novel, and did.

Update: Last year I received a card from the Third Millennium Writer's Conference asking for a submission to their contest. I sent five short chapters from this first novel. I never heard from them, which means rejection. They said if you were one of the top ten, they would let you know. I guess I wasn't. They were looking for movie material or short stories. It was surprising to get a letter from Francis Ford Coppola requesting a submission. I hoped it meant something—but, of course, it didn't. So I sent chapters of this novel, written by a 20-year—old girl fresh out of college, and it was called <u>Suns of Darkness</u>. It was probably one of the first Holocaust stories written in the U.S., but I didn't know it at the time. I showed it to only one publisher and to my agent, both of whom turned it down.

Adana's father Andrew died in 1960 at the age of sixty, and Evvie, her mother, died in 2005 at the age of 102. Adana's brother Bentley died in 2003 and my mother passed away in 2005 at 97.

Chapter 7

SLUM ROOFS UNDER THE STARS

I often dreamed of living in one of those big houses I sometimes passed on trains to Connecticut or Massachusetts. I dreamed of coming down a staircase in a long, beautiful gown and being ravishingly attractive. The staircase in the tenement I lived in didn't quite have star quality. I remember racing up the flights of steps until I got to the top. Sometimes I went up to the roof of the slum I was born into to look at the stars and to dream above the tenement rooftops.

A lot of us had dreams and some of them came true. I remember the boy growing up downstairs in the apartment below ours. He was in college and he wanted desperately to be in college, but his father wanted him to be a textile cutter like he was. His mother sneaked out to baby sit and earn money to help him go through a city college. Many years later I was so happy to read that he had been appointed chancellor of a large university. He had dreamed and so effectively that he dreamt his way right out of the ghetto and into the middle class. The stars were pointed right in his direction.

My dreams were in another firmament. I didn't know it then. But it took many years to put my puzzled dreams together and the shattered remnants of my scattered soul that unfortunately clung tenaciously to many years of dreaming.

Here I was today, a vibrant, young woman with a college degree granted by an ivy league college for women. I had been given a scholarship and while there had made a name for myself as a hardworking young artist. Inside myself, I was a bundle of assorted terrors ready to explode with fear. Outside, I was in my early twenties, having climbed out of the ghetto and I had even proven that I had a mind.

Hadn't I spent weekends in Darien, Connecticut with other college classmates, getting loaded at parties with famous people, rubbing shoulders with all sorts of "names." It even got so bad that I could only afford to buy the books of people I knew.

I, the little twelve-year-old who once walked along Riverside Drive and looked up at the huge apartment buildings, looked at the splendid uniformed doormen and wondered what it would be like to live in those buildings. I dreamed wild and elaborate dreams. Here and now, I was chatting with a group of intellectuals as I heard the names of many celebrities mentioned in their conversation.

"Oh, I was with *what's-her-name* last week."

"Yes, I got a letter from *you-know-who*—he's in Europe and his painting is going badly. He is quite unhappy."

"At last," I thought, "I've really made it."

Chapter 8

SNOWY VERMONT WINTER

I had worked all week for a magazine in New York City and this afternoon I was on a train to Vermont. I was to meet Adana's brother there for the weekend. We had been dating for a year and soon he was to become my husband.

It had been a snowy winter. I sat alone in the train holding my book and looking out the window. The snow-filled New England countryside rushed past the windows of the train and I could see little puffs of soft and frothy snow as I looked out. There were deep tracks in the soft snow, with shadows and gullies beside the tracks as the train sped to Vermont.

Leafless trees stood black against the night sky which had turned magenta as the sun slowly set. I had graduated from Bennington College and coming to New England now reminded me of my years at the girls' college I had attended on a scholarship. But now I was on my way to meet my fiancé.

It was late afternoon, the sun was going down and the shadows along the sides of the tracks were getting darker. As I sat on the soft seat in the train lounge sipping a glass of wine with dinner, I kept watching the shadows deepen as the train traveled farther and farther away from New York City. We kept heading up into the mountains. As the shadows lengthened and grew larger and larger, the sky had turned from pink to lavender to blue, growing darker and darker with each passing mile.

Soon, tiny lights came on all over the hills we passed as people in their houses began to turn on their lamps. The sky now turned inky blue and the stars shone crystalline in the night sky. I saw the dark, country houses light up as I watched the moon's reflected light on icicles hanging from branches of bare, winter trees.

Having finally graduated from college and now working on a magazine, memories of tenements and ugly, hopeless poverty-ridden slums were disappearing from my psyche. I was losing the memory of feeling at the bottom of the social strata and how impossible it had been for me to experience human dignity when I was a child. Children aren't fooled; impoverished children know their place as they know how to breathe. It isn't easy to instill hope in a poor child because they have learned their lessons well, every day of their lives. When told hopeful stories, they bitterly turn against you, thinking, "What do you know? Only those who have experienced this can really know."

Looking out the train window, I put down the wine glass that I was drinking from and lit a cigarette. Memories flooded back from my childhood as a Hasidic little girl wearing a head scarf and heavy lisle stockings, always carrying piles of library books back and forth from the local library. I visited everywhere in my books. I always ended up in the Orient. Pearl Buck's books haunted me and I also read Lin Yu-t'ang voraciously. The people of the East seemed to have the same joys, sorrows and dreams that the people in my life had. I lost myself in these books and waited impatiently for my future life to begin.

I put out the cigarette and finished my drink. In ten minutes, I would be in the Vermont town where I was going skiing with Adana's brother for the weekend.

Chapter 9

CHIEF PROSECUTOR

I've had a strange life. It's important for me to go back to the first days when I used to wheel this large, shiny brown baby carriage with my first born inside it. Often, when we walked to Riverside Drive to visit with Bentley's parents, we used to stop to chat with Dr. Jacob Robinson and his wife or daughter. I remember hearing them congratulate us on our handsome, dark—eyed son who gurgled and made all kinds of sounds inside his high-wheeled carriage which almost looked like a chariot.

They were usually taking their daily stroll outside, dressed in warm, tweed winter wool coats. We often met them on our strolls with our new infant. As the baby got older, he sat up in the carriage wearing his bright blue winter ski suit and hood that surrounded his round, little face. He was very alert and said "Hi!" to all the people who greeted him.

Many times we bumped into the Robinsons or their daughter. I have forgotten her name, but she was always cordial and attentive to us and the baby. I only knew these people as the neighbors of my in-laws and that they had all lived in this gracious Stanford-White-designed building on Riverside Drive for more than twenty years.

The building bellied out over the Hudson River and with all the window seats around the living room, we caught glimpses of many remarkable sunsets over the Hudson River.

It was a very cordial neighborhood along Riverside Drive in the West Eighties and it reminded me of Vienna's *Ringstrasse.* There were many famous musicians, journalists, actors and authors who lived in the neighborhood. Lenny Bernstein lived a few blocks down from us. Harry Belafonte bought a building on West End Avenue that was converted into a coop. The kitchens in that building were so large you could have a roller skating rink in it. He cooped the apartment building and my friend Rena bought a huge apartment for $30,000 dollars and lived there with her children until her husband was transferred to Washington, D.C. In our apartment building on West End Avenue our children used to play together running back and forth between our apartments. They were all toddlers under five at the time.

One day a new neighbor moved in on our floor. It was Lee Grant, the well—known actress. As I rode up on the elevator with her, she was with a man who looked to me like the French actor, Charles Boyer, but he actually turned out to be George C. Scott who later played General Patton. Another neighbor in the building worked at City Center and we often babysat her two little ones when she was busy at the theater. We were always busy with all the children running back and forth from our apartments to play with each other.

Two Viennese ladies lived next door to me and were friends of Leopold Stokowski who founded the American Symphony Orchestra. These women had a leather glove factory in Europe and sold their high-end products in the United States. When they were home in their apartment they spent time with their close friend, the pianist Ray Lev, who lived in the corner apartment. One day she committed suicide, and it was very sad. After Ray Lev died, however, Rena was able to get her apartment, which she really needed. She arrived with a three year old, a pair of one-year-old twins and a baby on the way.

After Lee Grant moved in, I tried to go out one day and there were cameras in the hallways. As I opened my door, a movie director shouted, "Please stay inside, we're filming a scene from our movie. We'll knock on your door when the scene is shot and you can come out."

I rolled the baby carriage back inside, a bit surprised to be living on a movie set, and laughed. Fortunately we had this huge apartment, with light and windows all around. My children each had their own bedrooms with a bathroom between them. They could play for hours in this apartment. The wooden floors were parquet and the ceilings had jets from the gas light era that had been sealed off when electricity was put in the building.

We had three large bedrooms and a smaller maid's bedroom with a bathroom where we kept the washer and dryer. We had a hallway as large as a living room and also a dining room, a living room, a kitchen and master bedroom suite with walk-in closet and bathroom suite and we paid two hundred dollars a month because the building was rent controlled.

The landlord didn't work too hard at keeping up the building and when Rena's ceiling collapsed into her children's cribs, the Housing Commissioner rolled back their rent to $120 a month.

The world is very different today. After a few years they cut up all the large apartments and turned them into studios or one-bedrooms and they charged exorbitant rents for these tiny, little rabbit warrens. The whole neighborhood changed and most of us either moved to houses outside the city or had to buy large apartments that had been cooped. The end of an era passed quietly by and almost went unnoticed.

I guess I took for granted the many times we walked up Broadway and bumped into a grey-haired man from Columbia University and conversations like these took place as if this was normal:

"Hello, Lionel, how are you?"

"Fine, how are you, Bentley?"

Lionel Trilling and his wife Adana had been friends for years with Bentley's parents. They even named their daughter after his wife. The upper West Side remained like a small village where most people knew each other over many, many years.

Strange as it may seem, over the many years as my children grew from infants to toddlers and then went to pre-school, I had never known who Dr. Robinson was until many years after I had left the city and was living in another state. As I turned to a reference in a book called *And the Crooked Shall Be Made Straight*, I found out who Dr. Jacob Robinson really was. By this time, my children were out of college and living far away in other states.

It suddenly dawned on me that Dr. Jacob Robinson whom I had said 'Hello' to so many times had been the chief U. S. Prosecutor at the Nuremberg trials and the person who dispensed justice to the Nazi leaders of the Holocaust. It is a strange and amazing concept to meet a gentle, peaceful neighbor whose greatest gift to humanity had been the dispensation of justice to the Nazis after World War II. I was so glad to have met this man and his family on the Upper West Side so many, many times when my children were so very young.

What a small world this is! And to meet such a heroic soul as Dr. Robinson was indeed a privilege.

Chapter 10

BURYING ANDREW: A CHILL WIND BLOWS
ACROSS THE CEMETERY

They went to the cemetery. Adana put flowers on her father's grave. Bentley's mother laid down a pine bough. It was freezing out in the hills, and you could feel the wind running through your coat sleeves. His mother and sister were weeping. He was sobbing. The two women were etched in black like two dark shadows against the pale, blue sky. The cemetery grave stones stretched out for miles and miles as gusts of wind blew between the grave sites.

As they turned to walk down the path they watched a new set of mourners getting out of a group of limousines. They felt the wind blowing fiercely inside their souls. There was a dark, cold, chilling feeling that ached inside their bones. Adana and her brother Bentley turned down the path to leave. Their mother was a slight figure huddled in the cold afternoon. I listened to the clattering of heels against the stone path.

I felt alone and sad as we returned to the car. Bentley drove his mother back to the apartment on Riverside Drive. After this, we arrived home. My son was asleep in his crib.

Bentley, my husband now, often leaves his mother feeling depressed and suicidal. He has never worked out his rage against her for the past. His behavior in her presence is always filled with finesse, charm and courtesy. But when he leaves her there is a time bomb ticking inside him which usually explodes in our house. He becomes unable to control his anger at home and this continues for days.

I notice that he never shows his anger to his mother. After a lifetime of not accepting his feelings, he doesn't dare show his anger towards her. Earlier this afternoon she left her jacket at Adana's apartment. This same night she called Adana and told her to tell Bentley to bring the jacket back to her in the city.

She also called me and told me that it was the only jacket she owned. This was hard to believe since she always looked like a Bergdorf Goodman fashion plate which was where she shopped. Since she had just inherited a large sum of money, she certainly could have paid for another jacket. Bentley drove to Adana's apartment and then raced back to the city with his mother's jacket.

He returned to our house that night inflamed with anger. The sheer presence of his mother activated such self-destructive rage that it was almost uncontrollable. I became the target of that irrational anger and that night he became argumentative and threatening. He began screaming and banging his head against the refrigerator and almost put his hand through a plate glass window because of his anger.

I was horrified.

A short time later, I heard the engine of his car roaring as he took off. He was running away from his life, as his car tires screeched down the road. I sat at the kitchen table trying to retrace the patterns of his life. He was beginning to show signs of madness whenever he saw his mother, now that his father was dead.

I sat looking out at the dark night and trying to track the past years of our marriage. I had been noticing for years that he was moody, but now his moods were more violent than I had ever seen in the past. I knew he had an uncontrollable temper and tried not to provoke him needlessly. Early in our marriage, he had not shown such unkindness and violent anger. As the years passed, his depressions and anger deepened. I found myself with two young children and a husband beginning to go insane.

After his father's death the violence escalated. Often I found myself in terror as I listened in the dark as he shouted violent language and hurled abusive and cruel statements at me. I heard the sound of smashing doors, the crash of wooden chairs, and heard him attacking my possessions. One night he ripped up my paintings and smashed the frames. It was horrible. I couldn't understand why and I was in shock.

His mind increased in aberration. One night he threatened to run to the window and jump out. At that time we lived on the ninth floor of an apartment building. Many nights he threatened to go up to the roof and jump off. My heart pounded with fear as I tried to calm him down. Inside, I trembled for my children and myself.

In a stroke of desperation, we left the city and moved far from his mother.

We lived way out in the country in a treeless housing development near Princeton, New Jersey. His moods began to even out, and finally they almost disappeared. They returned only when he saw his mother. But in her presence he was a model son, only to come back home screaming and ranting and raving. Always saying after he saw his mother that he hated everyone and wanted to die. It was as if he became infected with a virus in her presence. His mother never saw these performances. When I told her I was worried her answer was, "Well, if he wants to kill himself, then let him do it. I won't be pushed around by him or anyone else."

He was amazingly careful and polite in his mother's presence. He never uttered a harsh word. I and the children caught hell, but he salved his mother's pride. Her lesson to him had been clear. The last time he had imposed his feelings upon her, she had sent him off to Round Hill, a mental hospital. He hid his rages from her only to wreak vengeance on our family. The tragedy of his childhood was now too many years old to change. It was a chill wind that blew in the cemetery that afternoon when his father was buried.

I recalled the ride home. Bentley was driving quietly. He was friendly and courteous as we left the cemetery. Everyone thought he was charming. As he steered his car away, anger was steaming in his soul, and within twenty-four hours he was socking his fists into his skull, banging his head on our refrigerator door, and screaming into the night, "I hate you . . . I hate you."

As I sat in my kitchen, my heart was pounding with pain. Tears rolled down my cheeks as I sat at my kitchen table feeling so alone and as if my internal organs were made of broken straw. My heart ached as I saw his father lying inside the dusty earth. I found myself weeping and searching for an answer. There was no answer.

Where had my husband's soul gone?

Chapter 11

FIRE ISLAND

The sand dunes on Fire Island face the Atlantic Ocean. Shades of blue sky meet the sandy earth as white, frothy bubbles lap against the shore line. The ocean's waters are dark and greenish blue, looking almost black from a distance.

My mind keeps going back to Andrew's funeral. I remember again and again how we drove to Long Island to bury his father. At the cemetery his sister Adana put flowers on his grave and his mother a Fire Island pine bough. The wind blew between the stones. Bentley's mother and sister were weeping. He was sobbing. I had a dark, cold feeling that ached in my bones and wouldn't go away that January day in 1960.

Almost fifty years later his mother faces the sea from her wheelchair. She is more than a century old, living out her days on the edge of the sea—she had always loved the sea. She used to walk along the sandy beaches of Fire Island with her big straw hat, her large, round sunglasses and the small red wagon that she pulled along with her groceries inside when she was young.

Now her eyes stare blankly out to sea—and I wonder if she remembers anything at all. For many years she lived on the Upper West Side of Manhattan. So when Bentley and I married, we moved to West End

Avenue and Eighty-Fourth Street. His parents lived around the corner on Riverside Drive.

This part of Manhattan reflected the shops and the little world that stretched from Riverside Park to Central Park West. I lived there in the late 1950s and early 1960s and gave birth to my two sons at the Flower Fifth Avenue Hospital. They are now grown and living in other states. I remember the children's clothing shop where I bought baby clothes and the drug store that delivered medicine if we needed it. There was a *Ringstrasse* of old apartment buildings, most stretching for a least one half block each. These old stone buildings were relics of 1890s New York City before there was electricity. The old gas lighting fixtures were still in the high ceilings of the enormous rooms built at the time. They were inactive because they had put electricity into these apartments at the turn of the century. The grocery store still delivered steaks, vegetables and milk into the century old buildings. Elevators were operated by the uniformed doormen who also served as handymen and worked in the apartments if they were needed to help with repairs.

Our cavernous Upper West Side apartment had four bedrooms, three baths and a maid's room. The large windows let in great amounts of light and needed iron bars to keep the children from climbing out.

His parents' apartment was very large and overlooked Riverside Drive and the Hudson River. It was a Stanford White building with a circular living room that bellied out over the Hudson River. I remember sitting at dinner and watching the sunset turn from light blue to bright orange and then to magenta with streaks of pink running through it until it finally turned a dark, inky blue and later only a shimmer of night lights were left blinking in the black, evening sky.

I remember the glass French doors that separated the bedrooms and kitchen and foyer from the dining and living room area. As we sat at the round table behind the gigantic Steinway grand piano, the maid Dora in her crisp blue uniform and white apron starched to perfection would bring out a golden brown turkey, gravy, stuffing, cranberry sauce and bright green Brussels sprouts. She was the widow of a minister in Harlem when she came to work for Bentley's family and she was well along in years.

She maintained that the kitchen was hers. She was their cook and the cleaning woman who I had never seen tidied up the house. But Dora fed Tigger, the cat who was now twenty-nine years old and very fat. He had certainly attained an unusual age for a cat!

Chapter 12

THE LUO GIRL AND THE KIKUYU BOY

One evening when my sons were two and four years old we were having dinner with my friend Francine who told us of the plight of about 1,500 students from Tanzania (then called Tanganyika), Uganda and Kenya in East Africa. Apparently, they had come to the United States to attend college and President Kennedy had airlifted them from East Africa.

What my friend said at dinner was alarming. People who knew were worried that some vulnerable students would commit suicide because the pressures were so great. No one realized that these young people had no money to stay after their first year of college in the United States. Francine said everyone who knew of the situation was worried.

We offered to help in any way we could.

Francine gave us the student list, with names and addresses, and we sent them letters asking about their situation. We received hundreds and hundreds of letters back. These young people were desperate. We also talked to the UN representative who agreed that something had to be done to help the students.

My friend Francine had been working with an American foundation that had sponsored some of these students into the United States including Tom Mboya's bride-to-be who was studying social work at a state university in the Midwest. We met her as she was returning home, she told us, to be bought for two hundred cows. Many years later I saw Amelia on TV, now the mother of several young children and the widow of the assassinated Tom Mboya who was a leader in Kenya before he was killed. She was serving as the Ambassador for UNICEF.

We had worked with the Kennedy Airlift students from Kenya who had applied to American colleges and universities. They were to be a new generation of educated and trained Kenyans who would go back and govern their country. We got word, however, that there was a young girl named Annie in a private high school in Kentucky who was very unhappy at the school. She was one of the few high school students sent over to the United States. I will tell you what happened to her toward the end of this chapter. We realized the students needed help because summer was coming and the schools they were enrolled in would close. These Kenyan students had only the money they had scraped together at home. They had not been sponsored except for a very few taken care of by the foundation. The rest of the students were on their own with nowhere to turn.

They were not permitted to work in this country because they were foreign students and were expected to pay their way. Many of these young people had sold eggs, chickens and vegetables and had been helped by their tribes to come here. But the amount of money they had was extremely limited and once they had paid tuition and room and board for the school year they had used up much of the money they had brought with them. Most of these students did not have the wherewithal to continue beyond the first school year. The schools that accepted them did not understand how impoverished these students really were and they offered no real solution to them. From the letters we received, these students were desperate and we offered to help them in whatever way we could.

Many students could not stay in their college dormitories in the summer and had no money for food or any place to stay. This was a terrible situation and the only thing we could think to do was to look for a place that would put them up. This turned out to be on West 89th Street near Central Park West where a Quaker Friends' Service hostel was available in two brownstone buildings. I spoke with the director and he told me to send the students to his place and he would feed them and house them until we could figure out what to do. So we wrote back to the most desperate students and told them to get a Greyhound Bus to New York City and we would pick them up when they arrived. These students barely scraped together the bus fare to New York and many had nothing to eat on the long ride up from the Southern colleges they were at in Arkansas, Mississippi and other points South and West. When we met students at the bus station, we always came loaded down with boxes of cookies and fruit. They had been starving, many for days before they left their colleges. It was not a pretty picture. We drove them up to the hostel where they were given their first meal in many days and also a bed, cot or mattress to sleep on.

They were told in the South that they could only use the black bathrooms and eat in the segregated part of the restaurants the bus stopped at while travelling north. Many students were incensed because they were already angry about the fact that they had come from high schools trained in the British system of education and these colleges had no courses that even matched their backgrounds, achievements or abilities. They had wasted their precious money on schools that gave them courses in driver's ed and simple English that they had mastered long ago. The only jobs offered were as migrant workers picking peas, etc. I told them to just say "no" and get on the bus to New York. This situation kept getting worse and worse. Now, not only did we have to find jobs for the summer at which they could work, but we also had to find them new schools where they could get the education they deserved and scholarship money for these schools.

By now we had received hundreds of letters from students desperate to get out of these schools in the American South. As far as students in the West were concerned, we couldn't even begin to figure out what to do for them. This was early May and a lot more students from Kenya would be out of school in the next couple of weeks. I was becoming very worried, but luck was on our side. By now we had about sixty students at the hostel when a national radio program called to ask if there were any Korean students staying there. The student who answered said, "No Korean students, but we have many Kenyan and other East African students here." The radio show was given our name and telephone number and contacted us for an interview that evening. The radio show was held every night at Mama Luisa's restaurant in New York City, and we went down there to discuss the plight of the students from East Africa. It was a lucky break!

As a result of the program the New York City Central Labor Council approved the right of these students to work in summer jobs all over New York State. Many students were able to go off to camp counseling jobs which not only paid them but also provided them with room and board for the summer. Many students needed sneakers and shorts and we were out shopping with these six-feet-tall boys for their summer gear so they could go off to camp. They were overjoyed. Others were given jobs in New York City hospitals where they worked as attendants. Just as soon as we shipped students off to camp, another group of students arrived.

We received letters from many organizations willing to help these students and now the hostel was housing nearly one hundred of them. There was one letter we got from a girl in junior high school who asked what she could do to help the students. She said her father was vice president of United Press International and we contacted her immediately. "Ask your father to write an article about the students," we said. He sent a reporter who interviewed us and then sent the story out across the wire services to every newspaper and magazine in the world. The Washington Post wrote a front page article that said: "Kennedy Airlift Students Starving in the United States." That front-page article seen by President Kennedy at breakfast sent him to Abraham Ribicoff, Director of U.S. Health and Human Services to get help for the students.

We received a phone call from the former mayor of Cleveland, who was sent by Abraham Ribicoff and came to visit us and see our files and letters from the Kenyan and other East African students. We showed him what the students had written us and immediately the U.S. Government set in motion three U.S. Employment centers for the East African students to report to, one in New York, one in Chicago and one in San Francisco so they would be assisted with summer jobs and be allowed to work in the United States. We wrote to all the students telling them the good news and they were overjoyed.

This happened because a little girl in Scarsdale wanted to help these students. Amazing, as it might seem, since we had been pestering every United Nations representative we could find because we felt this country had dropped the ball and would have a public relations disaster if they didn't do something. We sent telegrams to McGeorge Bundy, to Adlai Stevenson and to the Department of African Affairs at the United Nations. We still hadn't heard of any solutions from these individuals, but we were hoping that they would change things by the time the new school term began and that these students would be able to continue their education. In this time period, however, I called many schools in the New York, New Jersey, Connecticut area and was able to get many students into Queens College, Farleigh Dickenson University, and other institutions who offered scholarships to the East African students. The students were overjoyed because now they could learn at their own level. Their education had put them way past the first two years of college and they knew now that they wouldn't be wasting their precious time and money and would be able to go back to their countries and lead their people into the twentieth century. East African countries had been under British rule and in Kenya their leader had been under arrest. Jomo Kenyatta led Kenya after they obtained their freedom and we celebrated that summer because "Uhuru" (Freedom) could be heard as a rallying cry around the world. The Kenyans had become free and would run their own country. This was an amazing time!

Finally, G. Mennen Williams, former Governor of Michigan and in charge of African Affairs at the UN, came through with a program to sponsor these students. In the future, only students who were sponsored and cared for could attend colleges here in the United States. Up until that point, a student could go to the library in Kenya, write to any school, and if they got accepted could then go to that school. The students had been harmed by the absence of a program that assured the right schools for students and also the money they would need to finish their education. This new program was a tremendous win.

Yet there were still a few students who had been lost in the shuffle. I bet you're wondering what happened to Annie, the high school girl. We invited both her and Daniel, who was in school in Canada, to come and live with us. Immigration told us we could give these students money as a gift which would help them out, but we could not employ them. Annie was only sixteen and a Luo tribal member. She lived with us but was not allowed to be in the presence of a young man until she was betrothed. Daniel lived with us as well, but he became engaged to a Canadian girl who visited us and when they went back to Canada, we were invited to their wedding. They went back to the University of Halifax and were married there and finished their education. I was able to get Annie into Sarah Lawrence College where she became a music major, graduated and went home to Kenya. All told it was quite an adventure and we weren't sure we'd get the students the help they needed, but fortunately they did and the United States didn't have a public relations meltdown.

I met many students that spring and summer and one of them was a boy named Gideon from the Kamba tribe and he carried a beautiful walking stick with a lion's head carved on the handle. He told me his tribe were the carvers of Kenya and sent their animal carvings here for people to purchase. I was so fascinated with Gideon's story that I wrote a children's book called *The Tuesday Elephant* and it was illustrated by Tom Feelings who won many awards for other books he illustrated and wrote later on.

Gideon became a doctor and went home to help his people.

I remember many other students. One girl had once been Miss Nairobi and she had come to study. She had to leave her three children at home in Kenya with their father, a leader of the tribe. Her own father was tribal chief and wanted her to come to the US to study and gave his blessing.

And then there was Randolph who was discovered by Governor Rockefeller when he arrived from his college in Arkansas and came to

New York. Soon, Randolph had a scholarship in political science at SUNY, Albany given by Governor Rockefeller's department where he became an intern. He managed to achieve this on his own and the next time we saw him he was wearing a beaded cap and long, African robes. He came back to visit us in his distinctive costume and his smile lit up the world. He managed to obtain his own sponsorship and looked forward to a great future when he completed his education and returned to Kenya.

Chapter 13

THE BIAFRAN WAR

The world is very small indeed. I had worked with a friend, Roseanne, a British journalist to help her raise money for the starving people in Biafra. Roseanne had contacted Teddy Kennedy and he agreed to help in whatever way he could. He called Roseanne in London and told her that he had urged Lyndon Johnson to sign a bill to send food and medicine by relief planes to Biafra even though President Johnson was reluctant to interfere in the internal affairs of a nation. Roseanne called us to tell us that food was coming and she was coming to the US. She arrived with a little coffin containing a Biafran child that died in her arms in the war. I agreed to help her when she came to the US.

Roseanne presented her case to Congress and asked them to help. She had also asked the Queen of England to help and had shown her the coffin as she had shown it to the US Congress as well. I had seen her correspondence with the Queen who showed sympathy for Roseanne's cause.

I worked to help Roseanne to introduce the problems of the Biafran people to US leaders. When she came to the United States she asked the ambassadors from various countries at the United Nations to support the starving Biafrans. Some of those she asked pledged their support.

Chapter 14

SINANTHROPUS PEKINENSIS

It turned out that when I was in college and worked at the Wenner Gren Foundation for my non-resident terms I had worked next door to Father Teilhard de Chardin whom the director of the foundation, Dr Paul Fejos, had protected when he was denied a teaching position in France. Father Teilhard was writing his great books in a little room next to our office in a mansion on East 71st Street near the Frick Museum. Saranna, Jane, William and I were all working on anthropological manuscripts soon to be published. Saranna decided to go back to graduate school and finish her PhD in Anthropology in the Midwest. She was the first to leave the foundation, and that was in the fifties. She had been accepted into a doctoral program and would be working on a magazine as well.

My doctor, Timothy Rawley, told me he had worked with Father Teilhard de Chardin at Beijing Medical University, then called Peking Medical School, when he noticed the books I was reading when I was hospitalized after publishing my first children's book. I told him I was working on an anthropology book for children. He said that it reminded him that before he was interned in a Japanese prison camp during World War II, Father Teilhard had given him the skull of Peking man to hide from the Japanese invaders. It had been so long ago that he had almost forgotten about it. Many months later I read in the *New York Times* that Dr. Rawley had reported on the skull and that it was to be given to the Museum of Natural History. *Sinanthropus Pekinensis*, one of the earliest forms of homo sapiens, was to be brought back from the Far East. But it never was.

I was astounded at such synchronicity. For Peking Man was the first to use fire and also showed the first signs that he had learned to murder others of his own species. For me that was prophetic because the violence in my own marriage continued. I never got to see the exhibition of the illustrations from my first book held at the 42nd Street Library. I was in the hospital.

My second book was published two years later. I had to find a way to get a profession. I needed to be able to support my children. I was desperate, for if I wanted to raise them up and care for them properly, I needed a teaching job. I enrolled in graduate school and got accepted in the MS in Education course. My parents lent me the tuition. There I finished my Masters degree in order to get a teaching job, so I could be with my children when they were not in school on their summer and winter vacations.

I student taught in an inner-city, black school. By now I was in my thirties. The teacher I worked for as a student teacher was in her twenties. I was kind to the children and she tried to flunk me for not being a disciplinarian. At the same time I was also reading my books as a guest lecturer at libraries and schools in the Greater New York area. Children seemed to love the stories.

Earlier, when I published *The Tuesday Elephant*, I was given a scholarship to the Bread Loaf Writer's Conference by my publisher. What an honor—but my life was so violent I could not leave my young children alone with their father. So I had to turn the scholarship down. They probably thought I was uncooperative. Few people knew that my inner life was so ravaged with pain and terror. John Ciardi, I believe, was directing those sessions. Sadly, it was not to be.

After student teaching, I finished my MS in Education and looked for work as a teacher. I could not find a teaching job, but was hired freelance by a youth agency to work on a proposal for several months. It was an initiative coming up for funding for a group of youth agencies. The leading force for this was the then head of Health and Human Services that was at the time called the Office of Child Development. I never knew him then, but I wrote the grant and we received about a half million dollars for the youth agency that was used over three years.

I was eventually hired full-time and, working for the youth agency, I wrote and directed over 54 books in the next twenty-seven years, so many, I probably can't name them all. I was a writer for hire. Kenneth Burke said not to work as a paid writer because it sucked all the life out of you. It certainly had an effect on me. Later I got another grant for this agency for three years from the US Department of Education. From 1978 through 1981 I worked on this grant for the agency.

Now this is where everything I wanted was lost, crashed, obliterated—over. At this time the divorce was taking place and it was the most painful, hurtful event in my life up to that point. I don't even know why. I was raised to do the things I felt comfortable with—my children, my home—but I could not handle the confrontation and terror of my divorce. I had spent the first part of my life wanting love and now I needed to cut off my feelings. The world turned ugly. I was sick of life. I was totally disgusted. I wanted once again to be busy and not have any feelings; that was how I could survive. By numbing myself I would not feel pain and loss.

I acquired a shell for a personality. Everything was to be hidden. I began to search for the elimination of my beingness because there was so much pain.

Chapter 15

CONSTANT SCREAMING AND RAGE

As I listened to their story it sounded like a lie. The night in the hospital came back to me.

"Why didn't I force them to get a nurse for him? Why didn't I make them listen to me?" I said to myself.

They wanted to save money. They saved money, but they lost their husband and father's life. Doesn't it matter that they lost a life because they wanted to save the price of a night nurse?

I don't know how I will ever get over this. I want to go back to my poor family where there was some love and caring. Since his father's death, my mind collapses from my husband's constant screaming rages. My children cry and scream at night fearful of the loud voices they hear.

My little son, clinging to me, says, "Don't go, mommy—don't let daddy send you away." My older son pleads with me to go for fear that his father will injure me. Inside myself, my heart and nervous system are frozen in terror. I cannot believe the madness all around me as he screams, "Get out, you are not going to have my children!"

I close my eyes and see this image of his mother as a black widow spider crawling on the wall and I see Bentley drawn into this web of madness. I don't know how to escape. I see him as a child again, all those years ago, looking through the glass dining-room doors of her apartment and wanting to love her and wanting his mother to love him back.

I seek to stay aloof from this desperate play of madness and pain. The horror show is complete. Inside I scream with untold agony. How could I have been so foolish? I think of all those innocent peasants I grew up with who had warm hearts and lacked guile. When Bentley's mother wanted to compliment me she would praise my "peasant wit." Most of the time she called my by her maid's name.

The forces both internally and externally moved in a twisted spiral. Why had he turned the force of his rage on me, the person who tried to love him and fill the loveless world that had been his early life? Was it too painful for him to trust anyone? I watched my husband dancing towards destruction caught like an insect in a spider web.

Dark waters from the past threatened to engulf his mind. His pride kept him from seeing the web catching him. Soon he would be caught, picked up bodily and lifted right out of our marriage, our life, our family. The tragedy was that he didn't see any web, and even when I warned him, he refused to look.

I kept waiting for his sanity to return. For love to return. I watched it like you watch a child with a fever, hoping and praying for deliverance. I remembered back to the sounds of the sweet violins playing on our wedding night. I also remembered how his mother never gave us a wedding present. She waited ten months before giving us a gift making sure that her son had not married me because I was pregnant.

When my first son was born several months later, I sensed that she had been fanning the flames of hell. I felt angry at the universe. Perhaps I should have understood that his mother was not sane either. After all, she had worn black to her own wedding and her son Bentley was born seven months later at full term, not premature.

I was advised to hide from this man who could not control his temper and the violence in him. I cannot to this day even look at those events without becoming sick to my stomach, even though he is dead now. He died a few years ago. For all those years, I had an unlisted telephone and lived without an obvious address where he could find me.

Ironically at that time I received a letter one day at work from the Archdiocese of New York City explaining that he had petitioned the Church to become a Catholic. They asked did I, as his ex-wife, have any comments or reasons that he should not be accepted. I laughed until I cried. This had to be the joke of the century. I never answered that letter. I went to many groups to find out about myself. The first was Arica, then Rajneesh, then Est and Actualizations, then Scientology. All these searches were to find out who I was. I have never gotten over the pain of my divorce because I did not understand why anyone would engage in gratuitous violence—just for power.

But I wanted a divorce. I wanted to get out of this marriage. I was so ashamed that my life turned into this horror story. *I just wanted my life back!.*

Chapter 16

JESSE JACKSON COMES TO GREAT NECK

One of the most amazing experiences I remember started out to be a positive experience, but I can't say for sure how it really went down. My ex had run for the School Board and lost to a wealthy lady from Great Neck who went on to win a congressional seat after her election and service on the School Board. My ex had been hanging out at the Center for Urban Education in New York City and developed a plan with the Director to create a program for gifted urban kids, mostly black. He proposed to the Great Neck School Board that twenty-five gifted, black youngsters from Queens be brought to Great Neck for a year to study at the high school. Now, that sounded like a do-able, simple, good plan. The hope was to help a handful of urban youngsters who were college bound spend the last few years of high school in Great Neck to help them get into good colleges.

Well, all hell broke loose in Great Neck. The elected members of the School Board would be casting a deciding vote to see if they would allow this plan into the schools and the Center for Urban Education would research how well this plan worked for urban youth. Unfortunately that's not how it went down in this little affluent Long Island town. Suddenly the School Board meetings erupted into chaos with people shouting and crying and being carried from the room when they fainted. It seemed the children in the high school thought this was a great plan and they wanted to welcome the twenty-five new students into their High School.

55

Their parents, however, had a totally different viewpoint, and they wanted no one from outside to come to their children's schools.

The press seized this story like a dog with a bone and they wouldn't let go. The TV cameras came to our house and while my children scampered around in their pajamas, a major network was filming, "Guess Who's Coming to Great Neck?" in my living room. This TV newscast ran for an hour and covered the proposal made by my ex to bring gifted urban children from Queens to Great Neck in order to help them get into the Ivy League schools they wished to attend. There had been a movie called "Guess Who's Coming To Dinner" with Katherine Hepburn about a young Connecticut college girl who brought her black boyfriend home to meet her parents who heartily disagreed with their daughter about her choice for a significant other. The movie had caused quite a buzz and now this proposal was making the media big time.

After the TV documentary articles appeared in *Time, Newsweek, Life* and most newspapers around the country. When I came home one day to be greeted by two reporters from *The Daily News,* I just went inside and knew we had to do something. By the time the story hit the major magazines we were getting threatening phone calls in the middle of the night and threatening letters informing us of our imminent death. It seemed that everyone who had ever lived in Great Neck or graduated from the high school was now going to protect the honor of their alma mater. My children were threatened at the school bus stop and had to be protected by the police as they got on and off the school bus.

The telephone company told us to keep the callers on as long as we could so they could intercept the calls for the police. In those days, electronics weren't very advanced in these areas. So, at 2 a.m. you had to keep talking and talking to someone who was telling you he had several guns and wouldn't hesitate to use them on you. Being half dazed and half crazed from no sleep while you chatted with "crazies" from all over America was not conducive to calm or relaxation. Meanwhile the School Board meetings required police escorts for the members.

My son recently told me that one day after school he answered the phone. The caller said, "Is this Bentley Garwood?" My son, who was eight years old at the time, answered, "No." The man screamed into the phone, "Die, nigger! I am in South Carolina and I'm going to come up there and blow you away with my shotgun." My son, a little frightened eight year old, told me that as he hung up the phone he was shaking with terror.

Things did look bleak. The School Board member who had the deciding vote had his home and life threatened. He had to move himself, his wife and four children into a hotel because they threatened to burn down his house. Meanwhile the high school students demanded that these urban young people be allowed to come to the high school. This issue had reached such a point of hysteria that the clergy of the town held a meeting amongst themselves and decided to back the program. A rabbi, a priest and a minister all agreed that something had to be done. They contacted Jesse Jackson who came to town to lead a march with the clergy followed by all the people who endorsed the program. These people were mostly children and high school kids. The day the march was held the clergy marched up front with Jesse Jackson followed by hundreds and hundreds of young people. They marched through the main street in the center of town and all along the sidewalks were the parents and mostly adults screaming at their children to get out of the march. The children just kept on marching. It brought tears to my eyes.

In addition to having the police hanging out in my living room a lot of the time, we also saw the threats continuing daily. The officers said to me, "I don't think I'd want my wife or children exposed to this." They were very helpful but it was terrifying. My son recently said to me that he had been afraid of these threats and lived in terror when he was eight to nine years old.

Even though the proposal passed the School Board with a vote of 3 to 2, the proposal was never implemented for a variety of reasons. It stood on hold for so long that it finally died quietly, and the good 'burghers' of Great Neck could sleep easily and not have to worry about their property values. For, all during this period, many people threatened that they would have heart attacks if their properties lost value.

Now, thirty years later, Great Neck schools are forty percent filled with Iranian refugee children, and still the property values haven't gone down; if anything, they've gone up. The School Board member with the deciding vote was finally able to move back into his home and resume his legal practice and the town settled down to its regular business after extraordinary chaos.

The only other thing that disturbed this sleepy little North Shore town was, of course, the Vietnam War. Again, it was the kids against the adults because, after all, they were being sent to Vietnam and they didn't want to go. So a lot of stuff went on from burning draft cards to demonstrations against the war.

I remember that at that time my children were quite young, about nine and eleven. One night a group of kids held a demonstration against the war at the post office. Most of the kids were under sixteen and there was a cordon of policemen protecting them from a huge group of very large and wide older men who were fighting to push the police out of the way and to get those children who were sitting down in front of this little post office. These guys were very red-faced and angry at these kids and they kept trying to bust up the police line to get at the children. It almost reminded me of the parents on the day of the children's march through town trying to get their children and pull them out of the march by force.

I was standing nearby making sure my children were alright when suddenly a three hundred pound angry man burst through the police line and ran at a little girl sitting on the ground with a cast on one leg because she had a broken leg. This very large man running from the police stomped on her cast and from her screams it was clear he had broken her leg again. The police dragged him away kicking and screaming and I couldn't believe what I had just seen. A man, probably three times the age of his victim, felt it necessary to fight off a line of police to assault a little girl with a cast on her leg.

The police called an ambulance and the young girl was taken to the hospital. The angry men across the street just stood there and continued to face off with the police. The Vietnam War ended and now we are friends with the Vietnamese and trade with them. The boys who escaped the draft by going to Canada came home. Some actually settled up north and found a different life across the border. After it was all over, many pundits stated the war had been a mistake. I never saw that sixteen-year-old girl again, but I wish her well. And, of course, Lyndon Johnson bowed out as President of the United States because of the war.

Chapter 17

MY FIRST CHILDREN'S BOOK GETS PUBLISHED

When I got married, I knew that I was not ready to be a parent. This was not what I wanted at the time. I wanted to have time to write and time to mature into this marriage relationship. I was bullied into getting pregnant immediately. I did not fight back when I should have. I tried to leave—but it was too late. I was already a victim in this situation. I did not go out and gain any independence. I had a first baby and then a second. I loved my children very much. I was good at being with children and they were my little friends. All the children in the neighborhood always came to our house and played there.

When pregnant with my first son I studied sculpture with Archipenko at his studio on 68th Street. His wife was ill. He took care of her. My schoolmate, Bernice was his secretary and student and a few years after his wife died she married him. Now, years after his death, she is involved in the direction of his Foundation. When my first child was born I went to visit him in Woodstock. He gave me the cottage that belonged to him and his wife. I brought my baby with me and my mother came to help me while I took sculpture classes with Archipenko who taught me and the other students at the studio which was in a nearby barn.

A few days after I arrived, my new husband, the son of the public relations agent, Evangeline, who had represented Rudolph Valentino and the Museum of Modern Art, came up and demanded that my mother and I and my baby leave. He threw a temper tantrum and wouldn't let me continue to study sculpture. I had been offered a fellowship at Bennington College to obtain a master's degree in sculpture. I had turned it down because I wanted to write. Sculpture was an avocation, I thought, and I couldn't see staying at an all-girls' school for another year. So, I left.

Big mistake. I wasn't ready for the real world. I needed to stay there a while longer. My sculpture teacher believed in me. He had my work exhibited all over the country. I also painted and watched my father's *angst* at his life because he had always wanted to become a painter. I couldn't really put any of this together.

The literature department had not let me write a novel for my senior thesis for graduation. They wanted a critical thesis. As reported earlier, I did one on Dostoevsky's *The Idiot*. Shades of Sylvia Plath's work on Dostoevsky. When I left Bennington College, I wanted to become who I really was. I was going to write a novel. I did. But then, many years later, I showed it to my literary agents. They turned it down. It was the story of Holocaust survivors—my cousin Carl and his wife Tanya.

Later, the brother of one of the agents wrote a teen novel using my material. He won a prize for it. The story was pretty much what I had shown them. I had also outlined a book on primitive art and the agent told me the publisher had liked my outline so much that he decided to write the book himself. I certainly was introduced to the sleaze factor early in my career.

In 1968, my first children's book was accepted for publication. I signed contracts. I had been sending my work out for a couple of years. The letters I received from editors were very encouraging. They said they wanted very much to buy my books, to keep writing and to send them more work. After my first book was published, I remembered one letter from a woman who I believed I had known as a child. When I was eight, I used to take walks with the sister of Norman Cousins, the editor of *The Saturday Review of Literature*. She used to talk to me all the time and I loved to hike with her.

For a moment I want to go way back, all the way back to a time when I was free. Way before illusions set in. Once when I was eight, I used to walk along the country roads. I dwelt in the shadows of the pine trees. The dark nights in fields under the stars were sometimes filled with joy and sometimes with strange shadows. At times I looked about the dark and the night was filled with fearful shapes—angry lions, wildcats—leaping here and there.

One night walking along on a peaceful country road, I pulled back in fear. I saw a black and white animal on the paved road in the moonlight and moved back in terror . . . maybe it was a skunk.

"I'm afraid, I'm afraid."

"It's probably nothing," said Sophie who was my walking partner.

But I felt overwhelmed with terror and wanted to run.

As we approached we heard a soft meowing—and there on the road sat a tiny kitten. As we passed the kitten stuck up its tail and jumped into the grass near the side of the road. I had had nothing to fear. As we walked along now I looked up at the night stars and watched the moon's shadows on the ground, under the trees and at the sides of the houses. Tiny, silver shadows flickered between the tree branches as I heard them stirring in the wind.

My walking partner was a woman in her twenties who was my mother's friend. We often took walks. I knew almost every pebble on those roads and often we took off our shoes and walked barefoot. That way you could feel every pebble with your toes. After the paved road, along a dirt road there was a forest. In daylight I would often stop to sit on a log struck down, probably, in a thunderstorm. It made a fine bench. I used to play games gazing between the trees to survey the large ferns that covered the forest floor. I counted the mossy clumps that grew around rocks at the base of the trees.

Once I followed a clump of trees and came to a clearing. I was all alone. It felt like I was dreaming. There I saw a shining lake with the sun's rays making it shimmer like gold. Drinking silently there was a baby deer. A huge tortoise came out of the lake. Big enough to be hundreds of years old. I ran away. Although this dreamlike sanctuary did exist, I never wandered near it again, and later came to believe I had imagined it.

When I walked along the roads by myself, I would rehearse what I would do if I met a rattlesnake. I tried to prepare myself for the possibility of a chance meeting, but I never had one and was grateful for that omission.

We often did see lots of snakes—green, black and yellow corn snakes, garter snakes—and as I got older I became more squeamish about them. Some days I would dig for hours for earthworms to go fishing. I would put them in a tin can and visit the lake in town to go fishing with the other kids. I would squeeze the night crawlers onto my fish hooks. I often caught catfish and would put my catch into a bucket of water while I continued fishing. I was very proud when I caught a fish until people told me that catfish could give a really bad bite and I stopped fishing for them.

If we kept going past the dirt road and the forest and came to the paved highway and turned left we would reach the Delaware River. All along the way to the river were little tributary streams filled with fish and many times we stopped and walked barefoot in the estuaries of the river. It felt terribly, terribly cold but there was only about eight inches of water flowing there. To a tenement child the opportunity to hike down country roads was a luxury that I dreamed about all winter in the tiny, dark apartment we lived in in the city.

Shades of green on the rolling hills along the road to the Delaware River looked like a carpet had been thrown up against the sky. Blue-green, yellow-green, brown-green and purple-green patches of land lay up and down the sloping hills as we walked along the roads. We passed farm houses with red barns and at last we reached the largest hill that we could climb where we would look down at the swiftly moving river. When there wasn't enough rain the Delaware just turned into a brown, rocky, muddy path with nearly no water and you could almost walk across the estuaries that flowed along the side of the road. The river was just as it had been for hundreds of years when tribes of Native American people lived along its fertile banks.

When we gazed down at the river, we watched the swiftly-flowing eddies as they rushed downstream. At the top of another hill stood a silver bridge. It was always worth the five-mile hike to climb up on that bridge and look out at the world below. I often walked these roads with friends and we would bring our sandwiches and eat them under the clear blue skies and watch the white clouds trace patterns in the sky.

I was filled with a sense of adventure when I looked down from these hills. Sometimes a train would race by along the edge of the river. It was this that I waited for all winter in our tenement. My summer dream could never squeeze into the tiny space of the slum I lived in—it was too large and it didn't fit there.

I loved the hills, the river, the sun, the lilac bush behind the old farmhouse, the tiny lily-of-the valley flowers I found on the ground and the Queen Anne's lace as well as the wild roses. I often picked bouquets of wild tiger lily and fronds of fern to carry home. I touched the orange, brown velvet tiger lily petals as I walked. I loved to lie on the ground reading between the two apple trees at the farm, and often when I felt hungry I picked an apple off a branch and ate it or sometimes one just fell off the tree and landed at my feet.

We lived with forty families in the forty-seven rooms rented every summer to the city dwellers who wanted to escape the heat of New York City or Philadelphia and breathe cool, upstate New York and Pennsylvania air. I never felt poor up there. I felt the whole world belonged to me. I would wander in the woods gathering blackberries, blueberries, raspberries, strawberries and crab apples. I remember bringing buckets of berries and apples to my mother who baked them into pies and stewed them into delicious-smelling jellies and jams. Everything tasted fragrant in the country and life smelled sweet there, as sweet as my young dreams.

The letter I received many years later was signed Sophie Cousins, and she was then head of the Children's Book Council and an editor at one of the major publishing houses.

Her letter said, "Please continue to write. If you ever feel that you want to give up writing—do not. Let me know. You have much talent and should continue to write for children."

Her letter meant a great deal to me. She would hardly have remembered me when I was eight years old and her summer walking companion. By now my name had changed because I was married. So her kind letter was sent to an unknown writer that she had never met. Her letter was so important to me—but it could not block out what happened.

When my first book was about to be published, my husband became more and more violent. He smacked me in the back of my head and I could not walk. I lay down for six weeks as the doctor advised, but still, I could not walk.

I called a doctor who had treated my son and he put me in the hospital immediately and then checked me for a skull fracture. He kept me there, sedated, for a week and told me that I would stay there until I could walk again. He was furious with my husband. Meanwhile, the pictures to my children's book, *The Tuesday Elephant,* done by Tom Feelings were exhibited at the 42nd Street Library. The New York Times reviewed this book along with one of its illustrations in an article on children's books about Africa. I had written the story of a student from East Africa that I had assisted when he first came to the United States to study. At the time I had worked with hundreds of African students because my friend, Francine had told me of their plight.

I had wanted to be published and I was, but I was in a hospital from my marriage.

Around that time I heard from Marian Gulbens, who phoned my parents and came to New York to see me. She told me that I had received the scholarship in honor of her brother to use anywhere—at the University of Chicago, Wisconsin or in New York—but the trustees hadn't heard from me and assumed that I didn't want it.

That was a joke! I didn't even know they'd given me that scholarship. I was also nominated for the Congressional Scholarship, but since I was no longer a student at the University of Wisconsin, it had to be given to another student. I never used either one of them. At any rate, I had somehow gotten through and Bennington College had given me a scholarship to finish school.

Chapter 18

COLDNESS AND CONTEMPTUOUS
CONDESCENSION

I looked at my present situation and wondered about the lies I had believed. I wondered what it would be like not to live with these lies any more.

I received a message that Bentley's mother was becoming worried about his rages. I knew she feared him having a breakdown because she might have to deal with the pieces again just as in the past when she sent him to Round Hill. But now she was a widow, there was only the inheritance, and his illness might eat up all of that in a year or two at a private hospital. So, she was worried. I was, too. I had two children to care for and to support if his mind went off the rails.

I never trusted her caring innuendos because over the years of my marriage I had had so many experiences to the contrary. I remembered when my oldest son had pneumonia and I lived way out in the country. I wondered why she never called in a month to find out how the child was. I know the price of a telephone call might have stood in her way because she was very, very stingy; but her grandson was very, very ill.

Her attitude towards my children and myself was one of great condescension. I didn't like being treated that way. With her sharp tongue she was always making sly remarks and snapping out insults and insinuating how inferior the children were, implying they were so because they were mine. When our financial fortunes capsized, our stock went down even more. She treated us like last week's garbage!

I did not recover from the shock when I realized rather early in my marriage that my husband's mother found both my children, myself and even her own son, too inferior to meet her level of societal expectations.

I remembered back to a time when because of a large financial setback we were forced to leave all our friends, our apartment in the city and everything familiar and move out to a rural suburb in order to recoup our losses. The children had been sick all winter with one childhood disease after another and my husband was deeply despondent and in debt.

In those times when I was able to visit the city she acted cold and unfriendly. I remember talking on the phone with Andrew, my father—in—law and receiving an invitation to come to their apartment with the children for a visit.

If we arrived at his invitation, she would throw a tantrum and tell us she had no food for dinner. I remember leaving her apartment with two small children who were hungry just as Andrew walked in from work.

"Where are you going?" he said, "I invited you to dinner."

I swallowed hard and said I had to leave.

It was then that I understood the treatment she had given to Bentley, my husband. I closed the door of their apartment feeling sadness for Andrew and leaving behind the door her coldness, condescension and sarcasm. As I walked down the street holding the hands of my two little sons, my tears were interrupted by an old friend who was driving by.

"Where are you going?" she asked.

"To the railroad station," I answered.

"Get in, I'll drive you. It's so good to see you and the children."

I didn't want my friend to see my tears. I looked out the window of her car as we drove to the railroad station.

Recollection of this incident made me realize why the death of Andrew had been so difficult for me. He was someone who always seemed to care for me and the children. When we had hard times, he always treated the children with love, not contempt. I realized now why I had mourned him so much.

I wondered what she really meant when she said that she was "worried about Bentley."

I was certain that she was worried about herself. For if her son could not face reality or the world on his own, he might be forced to go to her for help—and she didn't want that, not at all. Now, as a rather wealthy widow, she didn't want any bad publicity from her son. I knew she was busy figuring out all the angles, thinking her son was still a puppet on her string—manipulated by her sarcasm and cynicism. I watched this take place and watched him descend into a violent illness and break down. He became uncontrollable and very sick from years of her contemptuous condescension that left his soul in shreds.

I saw her as a hell hole of hate and like a seething volcano. On the surface, she looked impeccable, well dressed and coiffed and a perfect Radcliffe lady who had attended a Latin Prep School as a girl, daughter of a famous Boston doctor who founded two hospitals in Massachusetts. Inside, she was a smoldering cauldron of destruction. Even after years as the first woman drama critic on a New England newspaper, as a graduate of Radcliffe and a graduate school of Journalism, she was piteous. As I watched her son descending each day into the deep recesses of mental illness, I wasn't sure what to do.

Chapter 19

A STRANDED SPARROW

It's becoming hard to see outside. I'm sitting in my house in a blinding snowstorm and turbulent winds whip around me. Thousands of tiny snowflakes blow in all directions. Inside myself I feel the outside storm blowing in my veins.

My clouded brain feels murky as I stare out my bedroom window. In the storm I hear a tapping on the glass. I try to open the window, but a bird flies away. Surprisingly, a stranded sparrow looking for some shelter from the storm has flown into the increasing shadows of the night and has hit up against the glass. Somehow, as I witness this scene, I see a vision of a small child before me.

Staring out my window I witness a child planting seeds in the earth. A few weeks later the plant has not grown green or sprouted. This vision of the child turns into Bentley when he was six years old. He waits by his plant, but his seeds will not grow. He waits and waits and waits and cries out, "My plant won't grow because she doesn't love me! I want her to love me!"

He gets no answer. I see the dark green walls of his room crashing all around him. There is just a deathly silence. His tears roll down his cheeks. Golden streaks of light float into the window past the snowflakes.

I keep gazing out the window.

Chapter 20

POOR TRASH—DREAMS INTO NIGHTMARES

Now, things should be different. As I gaze out the same window a year later, my body aches with pain at the abuse I have just heard.

"Whore—bitch—get out!"

My guts wrench. I walk downstairs, out to the porch to cry. There is sun outside. There is darkness inside me. This has existed for a year now since his father died.

Why can't we bring the sun inside, I ask myself. Why does a shadow grow across my heart and numb it? My hands shake with rage. My heart is full of dark shadows and I am in exile from myself. My lonely days are hurtful.

I can't reach Bentley now; he is a stranger to me. Memories of past moments of love all translate into agonizing pain. I try to understand why he has ripped up our life like a piece of scrap paper. His mental processes make him a stranger to me.

On days when his mother calls, he is worse. When she's out of town, he gets better. I live in constant fear that he will hear from his mother and explode. After he talks to her he turns the full force of his fury against me. Vicious words fly from his lips. He calls me "trash." I try to forget his vile attacks.

I prayed for a kind word, but was locked inside his sadistic dance of lies. Bentley's mother had always been worshipped by her husband while I, who had married her son, had been kicked and lashed at constantly by

Bentley's vicious tongue. I felt like a fool. His mother's cool, calculating behavior never fazed him. Even if she lied about his inheritance he always forgave her. Even though I worked from early morning to midnight, he was always yelling at me: "More, more . . . do more. Why can't you do anything right?" I could only assume he believed what he said, that I was just "poor trash."

In my dark, lonely nights I wondered what had happened to all my splendid, young dreams. I looked for blossoms on trees every spring. Now my life had turned into one long, cold, desolate winter. My helplessness and rage against his nastiness disheartened me and turned my dreams into nightmares.

"What is this strange justice I face?" I wondered if I had committed terrible crimes in my past life or lives and was now being punished for these acts. My loneliness and desperation against his hostility wore me out. I was exhausted by his mood shifts and fearful of his continuing rages. I felt the cosmos laughing at me. I didn't want to see such a barbarous human soul.

After years of loving someone, I awoke one morning and my universe was scattered to the winds and blown away. After a long journey of many years, I had arrived back at the starting point. I had tried believing in this man, my husband, only to hear his foul-mouthed words resounding in my ears, "Whore! Bitch!"

I stood out on my front porch looking at the street. Tears ran down my cheeks. A lone car drove past. I walked through the screen door and entered my house again. Typing in another room, he had already forgotten his argument and I tried to attribute his viciousness to his hypoglycemia.

Chapter 21

EACH DAY A NEW SUN RISES AND THERE IS A NEW DAWN

Over the next five years my marriage disintegrated until it became threadbare. The irrational violence of my husband's eruptions formed a volcanic wall of solid terror for me. As he shouted and cursed us, threatening physical violence, I was left trembling while my life turned into a nightmare in broad daylight. Who could I tell—who would believe that this upper middle class family in Great Neck, Long Island with a Harvard University and Columbia University graduate married to a Bennington College graduate could disintegrate into this?

Most of the time I managed to run away from my elegant house before he could make good on his threats to beat me. When this happened, he went after the children in uncontrollable rages. It was these episodes when he attempted to beat and batter me that led me to decide that I must get away from this man. I had to end this marriage. I couldn't go on any longer. I was afraid to confront him with my feelings, fearing still more beatings and more uncontrollable rages.

One evening, Bentley as his usual insulting, angry self was shouting over trivial, inconsequential, petty matters. Somehow, this was the last straw for me. Something snapped inside me. I was through putting up with his behavior. I told him, I could no longer live with him and wanted a divorce.

He flew into a violent rage and came after me. I was terrified and tried to run out. He managed to grab my arm and knock me to the floor with a sharp punch to my back. I lay writhing in pain, certain that my back was broken. My two sons who were ten and twelve years old pulled him away from me.

I felt numb. In a state of shock, I asked my children to call Carol, my friend. But, I couldn't get up off the floor. I lay in the front hall numbed with pain and terror. Bentley went into the living room to watch television as if nothing had happened. Having successfully stopped my flight from him he was settling down to watch a TV program. I could lie there, even be crippled for life—and he was unaware that he had committed a crime.

My oldest son called Carol and asked her to come at once. Carol drove over immediately. As a social worker and an ardent woman's liberationist, she wasn't fazed by the call. When she rang the bell loudly, my son let her in.

She found me on the floor.

"Get me out of here, Carol," I wept. "Get me out of here."

Bending down to me on the floor, she put my arms over her shoulders and lifted me up. I was sobbing quietly.

My children just said, "Go—mom—get out of here, we'll be alright."

Bentley still sat watching television in the living room as if nothing had happened.

Carol slowly helped me to her station wagon. My children helped Carol put me in her wagon. I lay down on the back seat. Now, I was less frightened that my back was broken for it had been possible to move. My back appeared to be badly bruised. I was dazed, I knew I couldn't go back but I didn't know where to go. My children ten and twelve years old still needed me.

Strangely, I had known Carol when we both were children. We used to spend summers on a farm near Pennsylvania and the Delaware River. Our mothers rented summer rooms at a farm then, and now, we had met again after more than twenty years. We were both living in Great Neck, New York. She was working as a social worker and I was a research associate at a local university developing curriculum for a special education campus school. As children, she lived in the Bronx and I in Brooklyn and we spent many summers at the farm when we were ages eight to thirteen.

I fell asleep on Carol's guest bed. She had been separated from her ex for four years and she tried to be there for me. She was a single parent with two sons and her children were about the same ages as mine. That night as I fell asleep, Carol repeated over and over, "You have to get out of this marriage. You have to leave this man. You must or you'll be killed. Don't go back! Go anywhere. Find a place to go!"

The truth was that I had nowhere to go. "My children," I thought, "how would I take care of them?"

I didn't earn enough to take care of them or even to provide shelter and necessities for myself. My economic dependency had increased because Bentley took my paychecks by threat. I was terrified of being killed if I didn't hand them over to him. I had no money. I had struggled to save $300 dollars for my oldest son's bar mitzvah. After he found out about that, he took every penny I earned. I was terrified to fight back due to the constant threats he made against us.

The next morning wearing the clothing I had left home in the night before, I went to work. I forced myself to stand up and take the train out to the university where I worked. But this morning was different. My bruised back was a constant reminder that I was now homeless. I was in shock and in danger. I called my friend Janice from the phone booth at the railroad station at 6: 30 a.m. before getting on the train.

She had recently split with her husband. He had dumped her for a younger woman. She was more than twenty years older than I was, and very unhappy about being rejected after thirty-five years of marriage.

Janice was extraordinarily beautiful. With a glamorous, elegant appearance, she had lived in a large mansion before the break-up and until her husband had walked out on her she was always seen in minks and expensive jewelry. Devastated by her husband, she had left town and lived alone in another state attempting to pull herself together. The shame and pain had been too much for her. Recently, she had returned to Great Neck and was living alone in an apartment. Her two college-age sons were away at school and on vacations they stayed with their father.

When I called that morning, she said, "You've come a long way. You didn't feel able to break up your marriage in the past. You lived in fear of his revenge."

"Yes, and with good reason," I thought.

"You can't go back to that house," she said, "I won't let you. Come here after work tonight and stay with me until you can think straight. DON'T GO BACK THERE! He'll kill you!"

"Yes, I know I can't go back. But my children—what will they do?"

"What will they do if he kills you? You have to leave him to save yourself or your children won't have a mother!"

"Yes," I answered in a fog. But her voice was sure and strong.

"Don't stay in misery like I did. Get out. You are still young. Your life is ahead of you. Come here tonight. Call me from the train station after work. I'll pick you up."

I hung up the phone and I was shaking. In disbelief, I moved as if in a trance and got on the train to go to work. After the train, I took a bus to the university. I was in a deep state of shock. As I approached the building I worked in, the President of the university was standing at the front door. It was 7:30 a.m. and no one was due until 9 a.m. He always began his day early after a run around the 150 acre campus.

He had hired me two months ago and sensed I was a hard worker. I was given extra research assignments and the feeling that I could make a contribution to the university. I had planned to go to my office early and try to pull myself together before anyone came in. I was in terrible pain and as I stopped in front of the tree-lined administration building where I worked, I saw him standing there.

"Good morning," he said.

I looked dazed.

"What's the matter?" he asked. "You look like you have seen a ghost."

Tears streamed down my cheeks. I couldn't speak.

"Come to my office," he said. He took my hand and I went into his office, a long room with glass walls on two sides. One side showed the campus and the other the morning sunrise shining brilliantly through the windows.

He asked me to sit down.

"You don't have to tell me if you don't want to," he said.

The tears kept rolling down my cheeks. They felt hot. My back was scalding with pain.

"I can't go on," I said. "It's just too much. I've been living this way for years—hiding the truth about the violence in my life, trying to protect my children. I can't take this anymore."

He handed me a tissue.

"I just don't want to live like this anymore. My children—I love them so much. What have I done?"

He heard me. He looked at my face and took my hand with a kind look in his eyes.

"Come here," he said as he led me to the window wall brilliant with the sunrise. Foliage and trees pressed up against the glass, and beyond were lovely rolling hills with green lawns stretching out for acres and acres. I followed him to the glass window overlooking the campus.

"If what you say is true about all the pain you have suffered, try to remember that each day a new sun rises and there is a new dawn. Nothing in life ever stays the same."

I stood looking out the window feeling sorrow and pain, unable to think clearly or feel, but I heard him. I sensed his kindness and his gentleness. My pain eased a little. I had shared my secret humiliation with three people since last night. This was the first breakthrough in my inner system of keeping things a secret. I had trusted enough to tell the truth about my life and I found that people out in the world were humane and kind, unlike my husband. I could ask for help. This was the first time I smashed the insane system I had lived in for so many years.

"Thank you," I said and went up to my office to begin my work day.

Chapter 22

CALL ME IF YOU NEED ME

That night I called my friend, Janice from the railroad station. The day had seemed endless because of the confusion I felt. The pain in my back served as a constant reminder that I could not go home again.

When I reached Janice, she asked, "How do you feel?"

I couldn't answer. "I'll be here waiting for you," I said.

Shortly after, a blue station wagon pulled up near the train station. I got in. I was not going home tonight. I was agonized about my sons. I wanted to be with them. My children had understood. I was exhausted from the numbing horror of my life. We drove to Janice's apartment house and after parking, we went upstairs.

"Let's make you some dinner," she said.

I wasn't hungry, but I forced myself to eat.

"You know you can't go back there any more, don't you?" she said as she poured a cup of tea.

I nodded with a feeling of nausea welling up inside the pit of my stomach. I had no words for what was happening to me. There was nothing to hold onto, my life was crashing all around me and I felt like I was drowning. I must have looked dazed. Everything inside me was churning in agony.

"You know you can stay here indefinitely," she said. "Until you can figure out what to do, you will have to see a lawyer and end this marriage. You can't go on this way."

It was all so new. I never faced the finality of my marriage ending.

I was terrified of finding a lawyer and demanding an agreement from my husband, but I had no other choice open to me. I gazed at the bright blue draperies that led out to the terrace. The pale blue walls of the apartment and the carpet covering the floor which was a deep royal blue with swirls of green all seemed to flow together. But everything inside myself was spinning around like a top. Light filtered through the fiberglass drapes, and I stared at it. I was in so much pain as I lay down on the couch. Dazed, I began to fall asleep when Janice shook me.

"You need to get past the pain in your back. Take a shower and try to go to sleep for the night in your bedroom. We'll talk tomorrow."

"Okay," I said. Then I realized I needed to talk to my children—and tell them where I was and that I wasn't coming home just yet.

"I need to call home," I said.

"Go ahead, but don't get into any conversations with your husband," Janice warned.

I dialed. My son answered. "This is mom, how are you Keith?"

"I'm fine, mom. How are you?"

"I'm okay . . . but I can't come home tonight. I'm still in pain. I . . . I . . . I . . ." The tears were on my face and in my voice.

"I understand, mom. Stay away as long as you need to. Jonah and I are fine. We can manage. You have to look after yourself. We'll be fine. Don't worry about us. We know you love us . . . and we love you."

"Here's the phone number where I am staying with my friend. Call me if you need me. Don't give dad this number, I don't want him to find me."

"Okay, mom, don't worry." He was only twelve years old, and faced with this terrible life we had, he seemed so aware and mature. I breathed a sigh of relief and hung up.

My friend had exhibited a great deal of courage by sheltering me. She wasn't afraid. "Even if he came to find you here, I'd just call the police and have him arrested. Stay here. Don't be afraid. I'm certainly not afraid of him." She laughed.

I wished I could feel like her, but I could not. She was nearly sixty years old, divorced and in graduate school in psychology. She was a wonderful, gutsy lady.

I lay down on the bed in the room she had given me. I was totally exhausted. Nothing in my life came together now. My back hurt all night, but I didn't care. I was safe with Janice. The words, "Escape . . . escape . . ." pounded in my sleepy brain. But it would be a long time before I could. I didn't realize then that it would be four more years before I would gain my freedom. The night was long and fretful. When morning came I went to work knowing that in the evening I would have to get some fresh clothing to take back to Janice's apartment. I'd been wearing the same clothes for two days now.

Chapter 23

IT'S NOT A SKULL FRACTURE. YOU'RE SAFE!

I trace my own personal liberation back to the day my husband gave me a karate punch on the back of the head. The craziness he had manifested in small amounts suddenly took on monumental proportions as I ran out of the house, in shock, into the snow-filled, icy streets.

I kept on running from that moment. It was from terror, numbness and disbelief. The next day when I woke up I couldn't stand up. I was dizzy.

I called a doctor and when he heard, he said I had a brain concussion—and to stay down for awhile. I lay in bed for two weeks, and every time I got up I was dizzy. The spot on my head where I had been hit hurt and tingled strangely.

I was sure this was the end of my life. My husband was now a full-fledged lunatic because his favorite servant could not get out of bed to wait on him. He harassed me and screamed at me, and that drove me into a frenzy of terror. The doctor kept repeating that I had to stay in bed.

After four weeks I called another doctor to ask his opinion as to why I could not move around without the dizzy feeling. This doctor was in New York City. I told him what had happened over the phone and he yelled, "I'll kill him—I swear I'll kill him! Get here fast, I'll get you a bed in the hospital immediately."

My husband drove me to the hospital in Manhattan and left me there. He went home to the children.

After forty X-Rays of my head the doctor came back into the room and told me to relax. "My only fear was that you had a skull fracture," he said, "not a concussion. You're safe, kid; it's only a concussion."

I was so thankful I wanted to cry. He filled me with tranquilizers and I slept and ate for a week in the hospital—for me it was like a hotel vacation. When he felt I was well enough to go home he told me not to worry because he knew I would be able to walk.

My husband came to get me at the hospital. I was going HOME! My home had been shattered by my husband's insane temper. I realized now that I was living with a maniac and there was tremendous danger. It was with terror and panic that I drove back to my house with him. It was now a house I was going to run from for years until I could escape from this maniac.

But how?

First I had to pick up the pieces of my psyche—I had to hold my head together, so to speak. I had had one book published and the only escape for me was to publish or perish. In my case it was a matter of life and death.

I felt it was important to deal honestly with my literary agent and tell him everything—my first mistake! For some reason, compassion is not easily come by and people often run in panic at the first sign of trouble. My agent sold my second book, but then all action stopped. I knew I was never going to earn enough money to take care of myself and my children by writing.

My husband was fast using up all the family capital in his indecision and confusion—not paying bills and copping out on responsibility. It was a common experience to have the lights turned off because he hadn't paid the bills for months. Sometimes I wondered how he managed to get away with it for so long. Between having the electricity and telephone turned off routinely—I knew I had to find a way out.

The way out, of course, was to get my master's degree in education. As a teacher, I could earn bread and still have time to write. (That was before the bottom fell out of the teaching market.)

My parents, realizing that my royalties as a writer could pay for band aids, decided to invest in my graduate education. After all, a teacher can always earn a living. So, I went back to school.

I was scared. I hadn't been in a formal education program for at least twelve years. But I managed to get in and graduate. They were good years, in spite of the fact that my husband kept reminding me that I was making no contribution to the family income, and why the hell wasn't I out earning money as a secretary instead of wasting money in graduate school. It wasn't even his money!

Since I already hated him because of the blow to my head which had awakened me to the most blatant form of women's liberation known to humankind—it is called STAY ALIVE!—I had to learn to tune him out entirely, as if he did not exist. While he spent his time screaming at me for going to graduate school and wasting precious money, he also told me that he was contemplating being a teacher.

"Good," I said, "We'll both become teachers, and we'll support the family that way."

My words were a total deception because they were just a holding operation. I was trying to figure out how to stay alive and still get away from this maniac, who was also a bastard. It wasn't easy.

Chapter 24

FAMILY COUNSELING

There is going to be an end to this book because I am tired of the horror stories of the past. They are written here only to illuminate the total picture of these experiences for others. The purpose of the exposure of my personal story is to help others who face similar circumstances. It is urgent to communicate to my peers, other women and men, the seriousness of this state of affairs. Tales that are rarely spoken about, but that remain hidden beneath false presentations made to the world by people who do not want you to know the truth about their lives, need to see the light of day.

The people I meet every day in my life today would be shocked to hear of the beatings I received in my first marriage. Many would be brought to tears. My purpose in writing this book is to prevent this state of affairs from continuing to be visited upon innocent women and children. I don't know how to stop it. I certainly didn't know how to prevent it from happening in my own life.

I would have given all I possessed not to have had these experiences. But that was not my karma, or destiny in life. When I think back to the outrageous incidents I experienced and seeing how little support I had from the organized sectors of society, I wonder about the countless women and children still out there. Silent. Helpless. Terrified. Unable to speak or even ask for help. What will happen to them?

My purpose in writing this book is to call attention to this problem. I know that if I, an Ivy-League-educated, upper-middle-class American woman who came complete with a New York Times society page wedding announcement, has experienced this terrible scourge, then countless other women have also had similar experiences and perhaps cannot speak about what is happening or has happened to them.

My current life is different. I am an accomplished, articulate, respected woman, but this might not have been the outcome of what happened to me. I might have ended up just another statistic in the morgue. My escape was both painful and difficult.

I remember seeking family counseling and after a number of sessions in the counselor's office with my husband, the counselor finally asked the wrong question and my husband went berserk and began chasing after me around the Persian rugs and yelling, "I'll get you, I'll kill you, I'll kill you."

The marriage counselor stood between us. He was a short, thin man from a respected institute. I cowered behind his black rocking chair, fearing and trembling at my own impending death, possibly to take place in a moment while my 250-pound, six-foot-two husband was chasing around the room in an insane rage, yelling at the top of his lungs. The short, thin, bearded, one-hundred-thirty pound, five-foot-four marriage counselor kept on talking quietly to this maniac.

"You are really afraid . . . aren't you?" he said to my husband.

I was trembling with fear because it seemed like a gross miscalculation to tell this gorilla that he was afraid.

The counselor didn't signal to his assistant to call the police.

My husband kept trying to lunge past him to hit me. I began screaming, "Police! Po . . . lice! Po-li-i-i-i-ce!"

The counselor kept talking to this insane monster, and I was shaking with terror. He lunged at the black leather rocker to try to get at me. He got my upper arm with a punch that almost knocked me out. I was screaming in terror.

The counselor tried to push him back away from me. I felt totally unprotected and in danger. I looked down at my arm—it was turning black and purple where I had been socked.

All my screams were useless. Nobody, nobody called the police. My heart ached. Finally my husband ran out of the office.

The psychiatric counselor locked the door.

"Why didn't you call the police?" I asked.

He didn't answer.

"What do I do now, doc?" I asked.

"You sure as hell don't go back."

"Yeah!" I was exhausted.

I called my children. My older son said he would come with me. My younger son had to go to school. I went to the phone and called the police.

"I need an escort home. I have to get in and out safely."

"O.K.," they said. "We'll send a car—where are you at?"

I told them.

I put down the phone. I looked around the room; it was kicked around and disheveled. My arm hurt terribly. My mind was in a fugue of confusion. The counselor tried to calm me down, but I was shaking.

The doorbell finally rang and the policeman walked in.

"O.K. Are you ready?"

"Ready."

I smiled through my tears. It was the same tall, young black policeman who had been at my house before.

I cried all the way down the hallway.

"I told you not to go back. One of these days—you'll get killed," he said.

I nodded through my tears.

"This time—stay away, forever," he said.

"Yes, but my sons—my sons."

"Listen—if you don't get out, one of these days, he's going to get you."

I nodded.

We walked down the corridor to the elevator. The family counselor looked sadly at me as he stood outside his door.

"Take care," he waved.

The hall was filled with people who had opened their doors to find out what the commotion was about. Not one of them had called the police. Not even the family counselor, or his assistant in the other room, had called.

I had had to dial the police myself to get an escort home. No one had helped me. No one.

The policeman rang for the elevator. That was the last family counseling session I would ever attend with this doctor. He, too, had failed.

The next few years of my life were filled with bizarre scenes in psychiatrist's and lawyer's offices. The screaming and violence would never stop. I went home to my parents with one of my children for a while—but I couldn't stay away indefinitely. I needed to leave Bentley, but how?

Chapter 25

A GORILLA WITH A HARVARD DIPLOMA

The truth hurts! The horror of my past life hurts. When I take a look at how I chose to live my life, it really hurts. The pain in my gut is enormous and I keep running away from it. The wounds just bleed and bleed and bleed.

The horror of my experiences almost defies words. I don't know how I can transmit this experience to anyone who hasn't felt it. When I look at my pain, it is a wonder that I have survived. When I try to get a clear image of the running existence I led my mind becomes hazy. I don't even know how to begin telling others about it because my inner memory lies like a lead weight across my heart. It feels like a stone in my gut. If you have not witnessed this kind of experience, this kind of violence, can you begin to understand? Nazi prison camps in WWII were not that different.

Trying to sum up all the events would be like putting an elephant back inside its skin. The tightness of feelings, my inability to share my horror at the violence I endured with all who read this book—I am reluctant to tell about this horror. Others might not have reacted as painfully as I did. Many children enjoy a fight and when they win they are happy. As a child, I hid from fights. I tried to be invisible, I couldn't stand angry people, loud voices, people who didn't show love.

I feel a great deal of strain while trying to put down this section in words. There is no joy in these pages. I freeze as I try to remember a time

I want to forget completely. I am writing this for other women who have had these experiences but who cannot articulate them for themselves and for others.

Scenes are frozen and stuck inside my gut. Fear remembered is like a frozen icicle holding all my feelings in check. I remember hearing endless shouting until I couldn't stand the sound of his loud voice. When I hear shouting and loud tempers now, my stomach constricts and I want to run away and hide.

I want to run from angry, screaming people as I ran away so many times in the middle of the night because I could not stand the screaming and the threat of violence.

Never answering, as I waited in silence for my chance to escape if he got distracted for a moment, I would then run out the back or front door depending on which exit was safest to leave by. Sneak out is more like it because if he knew I was running away he would chase me down the street in the middle of the night, and it was terrifying.

As I ran for blocks and blocks in the dark, I didn't know what to do or where to go. At two or three in the morning my insides were shriveling in terror. My mind was burning with hysteria as I wished for a way out of this pain and agony. I prayed for my children to be alright. The horror and trembling would leave me shaking and exhausted in a telephone booth that had a seat and a door in a local hotel that was open all night. I ached inside as I ran through the snowy winter streets hoping to hide there before he found me. I was terrified of this six—foot-two, two-hundred-and-fifty-pound gorilla chasing me in the icy night. Once inside the hotel telephone booth, I breathed a sigh of relief. If it was before midnight I could call a local friend and sleep in the booth for the night. If it was 2:00 a.m. or later, I usually called my parents just to talk to someone sane.

My parents tried to calm me down so that I could think. Temporarily out of danger, I breathed a sigh of relief and prayed for deliverance. Sometimes I just sat in the telephone booth for an hour staring into space, sleeping there because in the morning I would have to go to work. The pain I felt was indescribable.

I numbed myself to my condition, to my rage and anger and humiliation at being driven out of my home on many nights into the snow and the cold and the rain. I longed for peace, but could see no way out at the time. I was afraid to ask for a divorce because I feared that would escalate the violence even more. I couldn't stay in this situation much longer because my own mind was about to snap from terror. At that time I was unable to support my children or myself and knew that I could count on no money from this gorilla with a degree from Harvard

University. I sat there in the middle of the night praying for a way out of this madness.

As I looked back to my childhood, nothing in my life had prepared me for this. My father was a gentle man who painted water colors and wrote poetry. I had been a gentle child who jumped at the sound of a barking dog. As soon as I could hold a pencil I had written poetry about loving people who wished to help others. I thought fighting was a mistake and violence should be banished from people's hearts and minds. But here I was on a battlefield being attacked as if I were the enemy when all I wanted was to love my children and my husband.

This paradox in my life was unbelievable. It left a sense of void and emptiness in my soul. I felt like Alice in Wonderland having dropped down into the rabbit hole, landing in total darkness. My fear was endless, the darkness terrifying, the aloneness inexplicable. I prayed for light. I prayed for hope to carry me on and to allow me to escape this terrible existence I had fallen into. For now, there seemed to be no way out for me.

Chapter 26

MY TEARS SHED SPARKLING, BROKEN GLASS

There are tears in the corners of my eyes. My face is full of strawberry cream, my body is sprayed with Eau de Love and I am crying. I am lying in a pink-blue pajama under a red-blue quilt hoping to stop the pain inside me. As I gaze at a white ceramic cup with a blue glaze trim on it, I wish things were not the way they are.

All the gentle, quiet moments that others feel are suddenly impossible for me. I feel a shrill siren screeching inside me as time quickens. I am running, running in a panic like a wild horse let loose on an open field after being penned up. I feel myself shaking, drawing energy up from my whole being. There is not a sense of serenity, but a sense of being ripped apart—of searching, flying, screeching. There is no peace inside me as I run and run in the wind.

I feel my body flying, my limbs weaken. I am crushed by the anxiety of my own divorce. My serenity has been shattered like the wine glass my groom stepped on when he married me. That wine glass has shattered inside me, and I feel the splinters running through my bloodstream—cutting flesh and veins, ripping organs, tearing muscles and sinews. O marriage glass—why did you break inside me, smashing into a million glass fragments, glistening in my bloodstream like mercury from another planet?

Luminous like the moon. Broken glass wandering inside my blood, my organs, and when I cry, my tears shed sparkling, broken glass. Did you know that Rabbis wait for young husbands to smash that glass? Young Jewish husbands who vow to protect and cherish and love their wives till death do them part. And my young husband smashed that glass too, but what I didn't know was that he intended all the splinters of that glass to crash inside my bloodstream and end up cutting up my heart.

I, too, can cry tears of broken glass splinters as I remember gypsy violins playing at my wedding in a Fifth Avenue hotel complete with a *New York Times* wedding announcement. Two more Ivy Leaguers marry. I was young and full of hope and optimism and sunlight moved through my veins before the world began to grow dark. This was all before the cold, crouching pain, and the splinters that moved through my heart muscles turned into the cold of lovelessness.

I wondered why and where and how I came to be in this place. A potential divorcee before Christmas. I know I am struggling to see through my tears as I try to listen to my friend, Mandy. Three glasses of wine at the Summit Hotel lounge in Manhattan have made me tired and dizzy.

"Mandy, are you telling me I am a free woman now and it doesn't matter if I want to let go?"

As I listen my head is spinning. I have become so frightened and all my feelings have shriveled. I sit and listen to her, thinking of all the people who still share passion and warmth and love, while I—I died some years ago.

I wish this hell was over. All I feel is aching numbness, fear and pain. The muscles of my body are in a state of withdrawal. I ache to sleep . . . to run away . . . twenty years of marriage . . . all smashed like that wine glass.

"Mandy, I see your face through my tears. I know you've been through the same experiences."

"You have friends. Ask for help if you need it."

"Thanks, Mandy, for putting me on my train."

I stagger onto the Long Island Railroad and ask the conductor to please wake me up at Great Egg, as F. Scott Fitzgerald called the town where he and Zelda and Gatsby lived.

I put my head down against the seat of the railroad train and stare out the darkened window at the passing lights. Tears are getting in my eyes as I hear a man behind me say.

"Wake her at Great Neck. You know it's that time of year."

I smiled, "Yes, it's that time of year, the time when you get your divorce . . . when your life is upside down . . . and inside out and backwards . . ."

"Great Neck," said the conductor as I felt a gentle arm helping me to the door. It was the man behind me.

"You said Great Neck, didn't you?" he asked.

"Yes, thank you," I whispered.

"It's that time of year," he answered.

"Merry Christmas!" he shouted as he walked to his automobile parked nearby.

Chapter 27

MARRIAGE WARS

It took me a long time to realize that my husband was psychotic. I refused to admit it to myself and rationalized all his behavior as the anger many people express. His irrational arguments were statements I always tried to respond to rationally. Having a low self-image to begin with I had placed my husband on a pedestal. Educated at Harvard and Columbia and from a well-to-do attorney's family, equipped with culture and a gift of gab, I could not permit myself to believe he was off in the head. Also, he was the father of my children. I refused to believe I had made such a mistake in judgment.

It was easier to blame myself and my own inadequacies. But the more I did this, the more he increased his bullying. After a while the only civilized relationship I could conduct with him was on the long-distance telephone—and not at all times.

For there were still times when he used the telephone to exhaust all of his vicious expletives. His behavior resembled that of a gargantuan three-year-old. It was impossible to shut him up. Going on forty-eight years old and over six feet tall, this incongruity was hard to accept.

When I first had my dreams smashed with an inkling that I had married a lunatic, I kept searching for causes. His mother abandoned him. His grandfather had taken him to live in Boston when he was an infant. He was brain-damaged by the high forceps used in the delivery room when he was born. There was a scar to prove it across his forehead.

He was all bandaged around the head after he was delivered. My heart filled with sympathy and understanding for his troubled birth. Now I barely have enough self-love to keep myself alive. With him I have been drained of all my own energy by a bloodsucking vampire.

I kept searching for reasons for his bizarre behavior and insane temper.

Maybe he was the victim of child abuse. He said the family servants used to beat him. His father ignored him. No one loved him. I had a list of things that had happened to him that went on and on.

I never asked myself why all my energies were poured into this person, and <u>why</u> I took such outright abuse. It was very difficult to put a stop to his bizarre behavior because if you reacted, he only escalated it even further, because <u>now</u> he was getting <u>attention</u>!

I tried to concentrate on my children by blocking him out of my consciousness. He never made much sense. Even though he could sound rational, his behavior was totally irrational.

In those years I tried to adjust. I became increasingly upset. After several years of this lifestyle I felt twice my age whenever in his presence. These people need to be shut out and if you do shut them out, you can barely survive, but the only real answer for this kind of person is to lock them out of your life and move on. After the separation, each time I saw him I wondered how I submitted to total fantasy and never faced the reality of who this person truly was.

I tried to trace this in my mind and see where I first learned about intimate relationships between men and women. I certainly had no joyful memories of my parent's marriage. Two people in a state of siege, despising each other for life was an apt description of their relationship. "Living together," they said, "only for the sake of their children."

Now both in their eighties with their children grown, they are still together and they <u>still</u> cannot live together. They have had their illnesses—heart conditions, high blood pressure, piles, shingles, nervous tension—all directly stress related. They cling to their illnesses as signs of their "martyrdom" in the marriage wars. They wear this badge of courage against unbelievable odds in the preservation of their dysfunctional marriage held together by their inability to confront their individual personalities and needs.

After more than fifty years of marriage, they had faced the world together unhappily all the way. Having witnessed my parents' model for marital bliss, it was possible that I carried the seeds of their distortions into my own marriage. In my case, confronting my terrible marriage was totally warranted.

In the process of confronting my bad choice of a partner, I discovered enormous buried self-hatred and self-loathing. To look at me, it was not apparent how much self-hatred there was. I wonder if there are a lot of people who harbor self-loathing and feel inadequate most of their lives. Feeling secretly inadequate and carrying these feelings inside oneself makes them difficult to erase unless confronted by the individual.

I had to face this abusive relationship and eliminate this self-hatred which I carried inside myself. This formed a mandate to CHANGE! Change is the most difficult word in the English language. How do you change? What do you change? When and where do you change?

Chapter 28

MEA CULPA

Trying to change yourself after forty is no easy matter. We have already developed these bad habits since our earlier years and it becomes almost impossible to force yourself into healthier patterns. When you have spent forty plus years harboring a secret hatred against yourself, it is nearly impossible to reverse that trend and begin to like yourself. You have to break old patterns in your consciousness that you may have considered survival mechanisms in the past.

In my case the impetus for change came with the blow to my head at the end of my husband's fist. It knocked some sense into me for I now had to realize that I could not stay in this marriage any longer. But I didn't want to confront this. I had to fight an extensive battle against my own self-destructiveness and willingness to submit and to give up entirely. An entire army battalion might not have carried all the bad feelings that I carried against myself.

When I opened up that Pandora's box, I didn't want to look inside. It just meant confronting more self-hatred, more self-blame and more terror and my lack of any sense of self-preservation. Why I refused to face these things is explained by the nature of the human animal. It's easier not to!

The more I thought I was changing, the more I realized that deep in the darkest, secret recesses of myself, I really wasn't willing to change. The ultimate secret I kept from myself was that I needed to SUFFER.

And there was no way I was going to give up eternal suffering, for that was my cross to bear! "Mea culpa", the woman's lot in life. I was a living testimonial to one of the major myths of all time: women are born to suffering and sorrow; women are born to bear pain.

I had incorporated all this into my psyche and I could tune into suffering at any time like a TV channel or a first-run movie. Martyrdom runs deep in the Russian soul and being a woman gave it Dostoevskian significance. I had written my thesis at Bennington on *The Idiot* by Dostoevsky and had probed some of the darkest recesses of the human spirit. I was sure I knew some of the answers to the human condition and wanted the world to listen to me. I felt sympathy and empathy for all humankind—every butterfly, bird and little child or senior elicited the warmth of my love for all humanity. But I hated myself!

In the service of my own self-contempt, I had done more good for others than I could estimate. That was dishonest because I had to learn to love myself first, and for me that wasn't easy. When we wade into the deep, dark corners of the human psyche and dust off the Neanderthal brain that beats inside our heads, we are greeted by our overwhelming primitive instincts.

Anxiety, fear, pain and grief exert full force. It was a problem to learn to love myself. Discounting myself was incredibly easy, I had done that all my life, while accepting myself was harder than anything I had ever had to do. I had grown up with the ethos that people who were out for themselves were grubby and grabby. But what do you do with an ethic like that when it backfires and you are annihilated by it? What do you do if kindness, trust and human empathy are not where it's at? What do you do in this 'dog eat dog' world when you haven't learned to growl and bite?

This gave me a new goal. I would have to find out how really angry I had become because I did not like being treated like a doormat. When you really struggle against your own self-hatred and try to let yourself exist, then you can gain awareness of all the buried anger seething in every pore of your protoplasm.

I know I was harboring a great deal of rage. I wondered how many others were ready to unload their anger, and if it all happened at once, would the world get short circuited? The grand design for us is SURVIVAL. Anything else was a frill. If you are trying to survive and someone else's heel is coming down on your face, what do you do?

Chapter 29

FLEAS! FLEAS!! FLEAS!!!

Since so much of my life is tied up with cats, and since I've written this book to be able to buy cat food, I might as well touch upon the subject of fleas.

Fleas are the bane of my existence. I can't wait till winter arrives so fleas can be temporarily disconnected from the cats. Actually, we tried everything—powder, spray, dust, collars. And still the fleas came.

Jonah and Keith were always scratching and screaming about their bumps. The covers on the beds were washed daily. The boys were never so clean in their entire lives because they showered constantly to kill the fleas. Years ago when fleas attacked there was still money to hire an exterminator.

For years after no self respecting flea would be caught dead in our house. But that didn't last forever, and I can't go back to the exterminating company because my ex-husband refused to pay their bill for years. My husband had a history of eluding creditors—till they were driven to drink. Conversations would go something like this:

"Mr.—your bill is not paid."

"Oh, I just put the check in the mail to you. You'll get it tomorrow."

Three months, two hundred letters and fifty unsuccessful phone calls later, the bill collector would call asking, pleading.

"Mr.—you <u>never</u> sent that check!"

"I'll have to look that up in my records; I know I've sent it. It must be lost in the mail."

"Please get it to us!."

"Of course."

It was with stunning regularity that my children called me at work to inform me that the electric company had just shut off the lights and asking how they could do homework in the dark. When the phone was shut off they weren't fazed, but the refrigerator and the lights produced panic. If the electricity was shut off before the weekend we had to wait until Monday to get it restored. It seemed to me a dim-witted way to live, but the only bills that got paid were when my almost-ex-husband got sued, threatened or service was entirely terminated. He was the greatest bill cop-out that ever lived. He had developed the 'art' of not paying bills to such a high point that I believe he could have been nominated for an academy award.

Ducking subpoenas and summonses to appear in court was another one of his charming traits. He developed the doorbell syndrome. When it rang he'd say, "You answer it, and if it's someone serving a summons, I'm not home—I AM NOT HOME."

The process servers got wise to that so when I opened the door they had already left the summons on the door knob. In this best of all possible worlds it is hard to grow love in the middle of a marriage that resembles the Second World War. My house began looking like the London Blitz, and personal interactions with my almost-ex-husband resembled a Nazi concentration camp with death chamber selections a daily occurrence.

What he couldn't enforce with screaming and yelling he enforced with his fists. I was scared to death and cowered in fear at his destructiveness. I felt like a straw house in a typhoon. I didn't know how to get out of the way.

I realized he was a drowning man and I didn't want to go under with him, but he was determined to pull me down along with him. I didn't like living my daily life like a Greek tragedy. My almost-ex insisted on Greek drama for breakfast. It started with: "You're depriving the children of love. Have you fed them yet?"

"Yes."

"Then why haven't they eaten."

"I offered them food, but they said they weren't hungry."

"Feed them anyway."

At this point I would stop talking because he escalated his yelling until he was screaming and shouting out my inadequacies as a wife and mother, calling me a bitch, a lowlife from the wrong side of the tracks, a mental case and general misfit.

When I began shaking with rage I'ld run for my coat to escape and leave the house.

"Where are you going? Running away again. Can't you stand the truth? Stay and listen."

I would stay only long enough to sneak out when he turned his back. I couldn't take the vengeful harangues that were wearing my mind and body down. I had to get outside and be alone. Nothing I could say would stop his anger once it started; he was like a motor going on and on without an off switch.

Sometimes he would block the door and terrify me.

"You are not leaving. You are going to listen, you no-good, worthless bitch."

Sometimes I succeeded in getting outside, and he would run out into the street screaming and chasing me.

I kept running down the street shaking until I reached the hotel that had a private telephone booth that I could hide in and call a friend before I lost my sanity. Sometimes I would hide at a neighbor's house for the rest of the day.

I was torn apart. I wanted to get back to my children, but I couldn't because of this man's insanity. I lived in constant torment. I would plead, cajole—cry—anything to stop his temper tantrums, but nothing worked until he played himself out.

Usually his screams escalated into suicidal or homicidal threats. It was Greek drama for breakfast, Russian tragedy for lunch and World War II for dinner. The great institution of marriage had gone down the drain in my book, but I couldn't find a way out.

Somewhere in my youth I'd been given the notion that women were human beings who could have opinions, feelings and even—heaven forbid—a point of view of their own. That wasn't the way the game was played in my domicile. It was more like "Me—Tarzan. You—Jane." Plunder and pummel. I often wondered why I had gone to Bennington College as a scholarship student.

They had paid my way and expected a bright future for a gifted young student that they had supported. My current role had disintegrated into one of a lowly housemaid. As my self-concept was being annihilated I knew I had to escape, but I didn't know how or where to start. My mother had talked about women getting an education and becoming independent, but she hadn't mentioned that somebody has to love their growing children and be there when they needed someone. I didn't know how to escape my need to remain a person and still meet my responsibilities to my children in these terrible circumstances.

My almost-ex held all the strings. Power and manipulation were in his hands, and I was caught in the double bind of wanting to take my children with me and run away. I tried to leave, but he was so violent and out of control that it was dangerous to attempt to escape. It was a despicable way to survive.

To the outside world we were a happily-married couple. The seams of our marriage were constantly splitting apart, and I felt myself torn to bits by his craziness, praying for a small moment of peace inside this maelstrom. No one can tell me that divorce is something people seek. It is thrust upon them by a series of intolerable obstacles which destroys their peace of mind and which threatens to annihilate their sanity and eliminate their sense of personal identity.

Chapter 30

"LET HIM CALL THE COPS. I'LL TELL THEM ABOUT <u>HIS</u> CRIMES."

The worst night of my life was when my children decided they had had it with this maniac. They confronted him with his evil behavior. I didn't know this was happening at the time. It happened shortly after my youngest son's *bar mitzvah*. My almost-ex was having his usual fights and my eldest son reached critical mass and began screaming at him.

His father said: "Listen, don't yell at me that way."

I started shaking when I heard screaming. I often wonder now how my nerves held out in all this desecration. I hid in my room. I then decided when he began screaming and shouting at me, too, that I'd better run away from the house. It was a warm summer night and I slipped out the back door to the garden and ran down the street as fast as I could run. It was too late to go to my neighbor across the street so I ran several blocks to the local hotel lobby and remained there.

After a while, I called the house.

My son answered the phone.

"What happened?" I asked.

"He ran away—but not before I busted his mouth. He was bleeding when he left."

I was in shock. "I think he went to the doctor," continued my son. "I told him never to lay a hand on anyone in this family again—as long as he lived. He tried to beat Jonah and me up, but we just punched him hard. I told him that he beat me up all my childhood and now I was going to make sure he didn't continue his rotten behavior, any more. The bastard beat us up when we were little, but now we are big—and we can fight him back."

My son, Keith was sobbing. He said, "Mom, I was so upset . . . I put my hand through a glass window in the front door."

"Are you alright?"

"Yes, it was a miracle. I didn't get a scratch, but I got so angry when he tried to hit me later that I really laid into him. I told him if he ever, ever laid a hand on anyone in this family again I would kill him next time. And then I punched him hard and his mouth started bleeding and he ran out the door screaming. Let him call the cops, I'll tell them about all his crimes. I hope he calls the cops. I hope he does. Then he'll finally get arrested like he deserves. He's such a coward, but he won't because he knows they'll get him, the bastard."

He was sobbing, my fifteen-year-old son seasoned on pain and horror for the last ten years. I felt paralyzed and exhausted. What kind of mother had I been to bring such suffering to my children? Their courage and strength were amazing.

"He'll never ever lay his hands on anyone as long as he lives—I'll see to that. I'll see to that."

I listened to Keith's sobs over the phone.

"I'll be back home in a few minutes," I said. He hung up after that.

I walked back to the house, my stomach in knots, my senses paralyzed by the pain of my life. I wanted to get out of this marriage. I was desperate to be released from this incredible hell. Having to negotiate a marriage separation agreement with a madman was like asking a gorilla to read André Gide. It all seemed so impossible.

I went back to the house and talked with my children.

"He won't come back," they said.

"We threw him out. Let him stay out. We don't want any visits from him. Let him stay at his mother's house."

Soon there was a phone call.

"I'm not coming back to the house. Did you hear what happened?"

"There's some smashed glass; it will have to be fixed," I answered. I tried to act cool. I wanted to vomit while I talked to him.

"No, not just that. They smashed my mouth."

"Oh."

"I just went to the doctor. I had to have eight stitches in my lip. I'm not coming back to see them. I'll be at my mother's."

"For how long?" I thought. I rejoiced at the eight stitches. "It's about time you got punched back, you punk bastard," I thought. "An eye for an eye—and <u>all</u> your teeth for the sorrow you've caused, you macho, insane punk," I thought. The world is filled with bastards who beat up their wives and children and never get caught.

"I'm not coming back!" he screamed into the telephone. "Go on welfare." He hung up.

I laughed. "Go on welfare." He didn't give me any money, anyway. What a joke. The only thing he did was pay the mortgage and that was because he didn't want to lose his property tax deduction. It wasn't out of any kindness to us—so I knew he wouldn't stop paying the mortgage. Since I paid all the other bills, what difference did it make <u>what</u> he said?

He was full of bull, and I knew he would stay away for awhile now, so I rejoiced. A few weeks of peace in this wacky world we lived in was a respite from this holocaust. I prayed for peace once again. If it meant kneeling towards Mecca three times a day, I would have done it. I would have done anything to get free of this albatross.

Chapter 31

EXERCISE!!! AND MEDITATION

Since the first day Gerard became my secretary he had been observing me. One day he said, "Why are you here writing this schlock? You're a good writer; you should be doing your own work."

"You have a lot of talent—why are you wasting it?" he shouted with sincere concern.

I was really surprised and touched. For so long I had had to hide out. My husband would tear up everything I wrote if he got his hands on my manuscripts. I was shocked that a total stranger would even notice my abilities.

In the twenty years I had lived with my husband I would have cherished a crumb of understanding that he would never deign to bestow upon me.

The world is somehow full of mysteries. There is lots of unkindness and cruelty, usually coming in little doses that eat away at you daily. It wasn't easy to live with a schizophrenic prone to violence. At the time, I would quake and jump at the slightest sign of anger. I wanted to run away, but I was in the bind of loving my children while hating what their father had become. He never accepted our legal separation and his neurotic games were all he wanted to continue. How dare an inferior doormat stand up to his machismo?

Aside from cats, office problems, broken appliances and not enough money to pay the bills, there are always those moments when you begin to think you are going to make it out of the pit. The term is transcend!

My solution to all the despair of my daily maniacal life was—EXERCISE! Somehow it seemed the answer to all kinds of deep problems I encountered. It gave me something useful to do with my body and promised serenity.

What I didn't realize was how many kinds of exercise there are. I settled for yoga, t'ai chi and kath expansions. They were supposed to put me in touch with my center, my essence. Since most of the time I felt like a wandering, dislocated refugee from suburbia with a broken marriage, the exercises promised NIRVANA!

I trudged into the exercise class with the others four times a week and put myself on a severe program of meditation and exercise. Anything to stop feeling depressed and shaky. I was a real stiff at first, but after a while I began to feel better about body movement. It was hard to stand on my head, but I was becoming expert at the cobra posture, the flamingo and the bow.

The group I worked out with believed in the unity of all humanity and we shared a common desire to love the world. It was just what I needed at this time to help me forget the beatings and the sadness of my marriage. It was a place where tears spilled and no one shouted at me for trying to be myself. It was a haven away from the pressures of my daily life that crashed in on me threatening to destroy my equilibrium.

I was wise to have joined this group because I gained the strength I needed to go on and learned to believe in myself. The original group had been started at Esalen and people participating expressed the kind feelings, acceptance and love that I hadn't experienced in many years. My home had become a dungeon with my husband always ranting, raving and destroying my peace of mind. With this group I could sit quietly until I felt centered and if tears came it was alright. If I couldn't keep up with the movement, it was alright, and most importantly—this was the first break I had made from the prison my marriage had become. This period of work and the time spent with this group helped me to put the pieces of myself back together again.

I learned here that all of life was a process, and that if we get caught up in bad spaces then we should try to find better spaces for ourselves. I found I could relate to others outside my nuclear family. It had been twenty years since I'd been close to anyone outside my family. It was here that I learned there was still love and compassion left in the world. After the blow to my head, I had lost all hope there was any human empathy left in the world. But I had to go on.

All the hope that had been drained from me had to be replenished. I had to believe that there was unity, love and warmth instead of destruction, violence and pain here on earth.

Chapter 32

"DO YOU WANT TO ARREST HIM?"

The turning point was a coincidence. I was always prepared to run for my life at a moment's notice. Enough psychiatrists, lawyers and friends had told me to go—but one day as he was shouting and screaming, I ran out of the house. He chased me down the block in broad daylight screaming, "I'm going to get you!" at the top of his lungs.

Fortunately, someone standing on their terrace called the police thinking a strange man wanted to attack me. The police were there before I had run down the third block. They grabbed his arm and wouldn't let go.

"Do you know this woman?" they asked.

"I don't know her," he said.

They looked at me still holding his arm tightly. He was finally afraid.

"You're hurting my arm!" he shouted.

The two police men ignored him.

"Do you know him?" they asked me.

"He's my husband."

They had seen him in the act of brutality: caught in the act.

"Do you want to arrest him?" they asked me.

I froze. If I arrested him, I knew he'd get me. I was frightened to death to answer. I knew he'd talk his way out of jail.

I hesitated.

Then I said, "No."

They let him go and he ran away. I stood there shaking and unable to think.

"Are you sure? A good night in jail would cure him," they said.

"I . . . I . . . am . . . too . . . afraid."

"You may be sorry . . . but we can't tell you what to do," said the police. But you better not go home."

I nodded.

"Can you help me get some things so I can get out of there?"

"Sure."

They drove to my house. I hastily packed a bag and called a friend. My mind was almost drugged from all this terror. I couldn't think. I just wanted to escape. Anything to find a moment of peace in this madhouse that was my life.

Chapter 33

MY FRIEND FORGOT TO KILL HERSELF
IN ROME: SUICIDE SCENARIOS

I once had a friend in my meditation group who told me that she promised herself if she had not married by her thirtieth birthday that she would commit suicide. It seemed like a strange goal, but these days who knows where people are at, anyway.

She had faithfully promised to do this unthinkable deed and I met her when she was thirty-one and asked her what went wrong.

"Well," she said, "I was over in Italy on my thirtieth birthday and was having a lot of fun. When I realized that I had passed thirty and was still alive, there was no point in doing it a few days later."

"Uh huh," I said, "sounds reasonable." I was a little puzzled, but she is a very lovely person, and I'm really glad she forgot to kill herself in Rome.

This suicide scenario is very rampant in my life these days, since I sat through more suicide episodes than I care to remember. My ex was big on suicide threats and they became almost a daily occurrence. The ritual began when my boys were in infancy and were playing at a friend's house. They were having lots of fun when the phone rang. It was my husband.

"I'm going to jump off the subway platform onto the train tracks. You'll never see me again."

I was all shook up. "Don't do that!" I panicked.

The whole charade ended when he went to a Chinese restaurant and forgot about it over sweet and sour shrimp.

I, on the other hand, had not forgotten about it. I was a shaking mess with tachycardia by the time I got back to my apartment and was expecting to call the undertaker or hear shortly from the subway police. I was surprised to find him in the bathtub reading the New York Times. He had even forgotten about the phone call.

I was totally confused. I was a stranger to this type of dramatic paradox. Of course, his suicide threats continued and escalated; by now, I had to call in a suicide expert—the best in the country. After a few months of treating my husband, the expert was ready to commit suicide himself. By now, I was becoming a rather sharp psychiatric nurse, ready at a moment's notice to counter a suicide threat with a nurturing comment like, "What will the children do without you?"

Scenes varied and the dialogue changed, but the pattern was repeated and repeated and repeated . . . on and on . . . and on. The genius that went into these concoctions could have been better spent stopping the Arab-Israeli conflict, but who was I to argue with his pathology. No one ever said I was God.

The most climactic scene of all was several years back when my husband ran to the kitchen drawer for a knife and screamed for the thousandth time, "I'm going to kill myself!"

Fortunately I wasn't home and my oldest son said, "Go ahead, dad."

He reported that his father went into the downstairs bathroom with the knife and let out a bloodcurdling scream as he fell to the floor, after he had closed the door of course. If I had witnessed that scene I would have had delirium tremens for a week. Fortunately my son has a cool head and he just opened the bathroom door and said, "O.K., dad, come on out—act three is over!"

In explaining this macabre episode to me, my son said, "Ah come on, mom, you don't really think he's going to do it—he's had a lot of chances already, hasn't he?"

But I always worry!

I haven't learned not to react—I've just learned not to listen. That saves a lot of wear and tear on my psyche. When I'm really at my wits end now I call his mother and she usually takes it from there. It's like having a telephone squad. Divorce or not, he hasn't given up his suicide threats. But I'm looking longingly at the world map to find a place out of earshot. I stick little pins in faraway places and murmur, "Someday."

Some women on the brink of divorce contemplate romance, a lover—I contemplate the map looking for a little spot on the globe where I can catch up on my sleep and live in peace and tranquility. At this point, several lifetimes might not be enough.

Chapter 34

"CAN I HELP YOU?"

After many months of running out of my house as the only possibility for survival, my nervous system was shot. I never knew when his anger would escalate into a vicious, violent scene. Sometimes he would just forget about what he was saying and cool off or leave the house a few hours later, seemingly normal again.

I never knew when the time bomb would detonate and I felt my inner reality constantly trembling like a bowl of Jello. There was no peace, even at quiet times. I plotted ways to leave. I needed to be calm and think, but that was almost impossible. There were small moments along the way when I thought and hoped that there would be a resolution.

The family counselors offered hope until he ran his number on them. He tried to punch me around in their offices, and they stood between us trying to stop him. He was totally unreasonable and it was always my fault that he was angry. Tears rolled down my face and I hardly believed that this was my own life that I was witnessing. It was with revulsion that I awakened each morning—never knowing what each day would bring.

If only there were some help, but there wasn't.

All help had failed.

The psychiatrists he saw either believed him and thought I was the cause of all the pain and fighting or they threw him out because he provoked them to rage with his unreasonable behavior. I wanted a divorce, but didn't know how to get through the dissolution of this marriage without getting murdered.

I prayed continuously. Life seemed such a miserable cheat and the joke had been on me. I had really muffed it this time and had added to the world's general misery by two more children, my sons. My heart ached for the two lives I had delivered here to witness this agony.

A thin ray of light broke through the darkness one night as I was running in the snow. I couldn't take it anymore. I stood near the railroad track deciding whether to go into the city in the middle of the night. I was clutching my fur coat around me, and the cold air blew through my veins. As I stood in the snow watching the shiny train tracks, someone tapped my shoulder. I had long since forgotten how to cry. I was usually numb with horror and just staring into space.

This time the hand that touched my shoulder was accompanied by a sound. In the dark night, with a few stars shining on the snow, I heard these words: "Can I help you? Is something the matter?"

I turned to see the face of a man I'd seen many times before. He was a local cab driver. He kept looking at my face. "I used to be a cop; I'm a retired policeman. Here, get into my taxi and warm up. Let's see if I can help you."

I was stunned. In so many months of running, suddenly God had answered my prayers. Here was help at last.

Probably a more sturdy, aggressive, angry woman could have handled my situation. But I couldn't. I just wandered around in a fog when these episodes took place and I prayed the rest of the time.

I kept looking at his face, not believing that a man was there wishing to help me. It was like Janus, I had only seen the angry side of the mask—maybe there was another side?

"Yes, I need some help." I got into his cab. He had seen me for years with my two sons as they were growing up. He knew about our two cats. He even knew what house I lived in.

I told him about my fears and the beatings.

"I know you can't get much help from the police; they don't like to interfere in domestic quarrels."

I was too ashamed to call the police; I didn't want to expose this situation and I blamed myself for being in it, but I didn't know what to do.

I listened to him in a half fog. It was two a.m.

"What do you want to do?" he asked.

"Well, I thought I would take a train to the city and stay with my parents," I answered, "But I am fearful of wandering about the city at three a.m. in the morning. But I'm afraid to go home . . . I don't know what to do."

He looked at me some more. His face seemed kind and caring.

"Look," he said, "Let me take you to my friends, the local cops, and we'll talk to them. We can't leave you unprotected this way—it will never stop."

He drove me up a dark street to the precinct which was outside in a little park. There were three squad cars parked near a little wooden building. I was dizzy and scared.

He talked to the police while I stayed in the cab unable to believe my life. The police came back and asked me a number of questions. One of which was,

"Do you want to go home?"

I answered, "Yes—but I am afraid."

They agreed to escort me home and to warn my husband that his behavior wouldn't be tolerated. I was numb when I got into the police car with them. So many times after episodes like this I'd gone home alone. This was, of course, better.

The police rang the doorbell and he answered. They took him aside and warned him. I heard him deny everything and call me crazy. I could certainly agree to that, for if I wasn't, then I wouldn't have been living with <u>him.</u>

I felt relieved to get back to my room and figured he wouldn't start anything tonight because of the police visit. Before the three tall cops left, they told me they thought he had calmed down enough for me to stay. But if I had any trouble not to hesitate to call them. I nodded and again in a fog, I closed the door and went to my room.

I tried to sleep. I prayed for calm when I heard him banging on the door and screaming. I had put a book case in front of it. He tried to push the door in, and gave up.

"If you ever call the police again," he shouted, "I'll kill you."

I cowered in the room sweating and trembling in terror. But he had gone away. I fell asleep exhausted.

Chapter 35

COSMIC LAUGHTER

The struggle for power and money is yet another snicker in the cosmic laughter hidden behind clouds of misunderstanding. After all, women have beaten themselves at both ends. They ask for less, and in addition, they are offered less. When both of these dovetail, we have the image of many modern women. Often women are certain that they are less worthy and will accept their role as a subordinate one in the hierarchy of life. Men who are also certain women are less deserving will make certain that women get less, and thereby assure them even less success.

I feel enormous rage at this state of affairs. What I can do about it is the following: have a nervous breakdown, sneak between the raindrops, ask for less money and power than I deserve, or FIGHT BACK! I am not very experienced at fighting back, so the struggle continues as an uphill climb. Did you ever see an elephant climb uphill? I see myself going downhill as a woman faster than uphill.

Even if I am a woman, the anger pours out of my consciousness because I won't accept second class and if I do, I feel that I've played someone else's game and lost. I want to play my own game and I want to have a say in how the rules are set up. I want equality, truth, integrity and human decency. I do not want false values that destroy creativity and the potential of human beings. There's no more time for that; the world will self destruct if it continues down that path.

Chapter 36

"WHY HAVEN'T YOU SERVED THE TURKEY?"

After three years of trying to starve us out, my almost-ex decided to be generous.

"How would you like a turkey for Christmas, my present to you and the kids?"

I never look a gift horse in the mouth even if is from a rattlesnake, so I said, "All contributions will be gratefully accepted."

Since the Ivy League tuition for my eldest son was due shortly, we were going into an austerity period again. But I smelled a rat. I knew for every bite of turkey from my almost-ex, I would pay in blood, or as Jean Paul Sartre aptly put it, "Nausea."

I didn't know how on-target my instincts had become. It seems I had learned my lessons well in the school of marriage martyrdom. Why should my almost-ex suddenly do an about-face and actually offer us food when his game had always been to starve us? Then the truth struck like a lead hammer. This day I had the misfortune to be in the same place at the same time as him—that is, my house.

The cleaning woman was carrying out the usual mounds of garbage, and I was suffering my usual guilt about having someone help me clean this huge, white, elephantine house. But since it would take me two weeks to do what she does in one day, I would rather go without food than give her up. My almost-ex-husband would like me to go without food and without a cleaning lady, too. She was buzzing around the house vacuuming and trying to keep her own head together because her unmarried, teen daughter had come home pregnant in the last week and was giving her a hard time. We were discussing this when a great shout was heard from downstairs.

"Why haven't you served the turkey?"

My first mistake was to answer.

"I have."

The screaming got louder, "I bought this turkey for you and the kids when I couldn't afford it because you said you were starving and didn't have any money to buy food."

The last bite of turkey I had had the night before started coming up in my throat. I wish I had vomited in his face, but instead I just got nauseous. The screaming continued.

"Why don't you take care of these children? They didn't eat any turkey."

"They did." My second mistake.

"You're lying. You are a disgusting lousy bitch."

By this time, I felt like I had an ulcer. Where were the boys, why didn't they mention they had had turkey the night before? I spied Jonah sneaking into his brother's room where the television was set up to watch the Dallas Cowboys.

"Tell him you were served turkey last night, Jonah."

"Yeah," he answered and closed the door quickly.

By now the vacuum cleaner was going full blast and you could hear my almost-ex shouting above it.

"I have to go out now," I said, looking longingly at the door. I needed air.

As I walked towards the door, I heard yelling.

"Where are you going—do you have a date?"

At eleven o'clock in the morning, I thought, a date? I should be so lucky. Actually, I did have a date at the bank to check my miniscule checking account balance to see if I could afford to buy the boys some jockey shorts so they wouldn't turn blue in their private parts from the cold weather in the winter.

"What business is it of yours, where I go?"

"It is my business—you no good, rotten, low down . . ." He was foaming at the mouth again.

I slammed the door shut behind me and deeply breathed in the out of doors.

Fresh air! I breathed in and walked down to town and the bank. Nausea was still with me, but I had certainly improved over the past when I would literally be trembling and shaking for hours after one of these episodes. This time I just wanted to vomit. This was a sign of progress in my psyche!

He was still seeking an Academy Award nomination for hysterical screaming. One of these days, I thought, he was going to make a big splash and I didn't want to be around when it happened. I've had enough high drama to last me for several lifetimes. I wondered what the cats thought of this. Our cats have actually grown up in a household with very little shouting because my almost-ex-husband and I split before they came to live at the house.

I don't want to recall the years and years of agony I went through just to get out of this marriage, but one thing is for certain: it scares me to think of any more angst like this with someone else.

P.S. I vomited in my bioenergetics class later because all that existential nausea caused me to want to throw up yesterday's turkey. Who wants to suffer human pollution? Living twenty years with a turkey was enough. Seventeen and a half dollars for the damned bird wasn't really going to put him in the poor house, and if he needs the money back so badly, I'll mail him a check when my bank balance can stand it!

Chapter 37

TO BERNIE, WHOM WE'LL ALWAYS LOVE

On the subject of cats, I have become an instant expert, the stimulus being my younger son's attachment to five furry friends, down from nine this summer. The cat syndrome began strangely enough in San Francisco when visiting my brother who owns three. One of these three is a stray who insinuated himself into the household by screaming loudly on the porch at mealtimes. My brother's two domesticated Siamese thus acquired a companion, an alley cat he named Thomas Jefferson.

When my two sons and I reached California after a cross-Canadian trek through the Rockies, Jonah was inspired by the cats' felicity and domesticity. So he decided to increase the size of his cat family. That's alright if you can afford to feed lots of cats, but when you can hardly feed your family it causes some teeth gnashing.

Actually Jonah didn't just decide to increase his feline family; this all came about through tragedy. Jonah had one beloved kitten named Bernie whom we left behind for a month as we journeyed West via the Canadian Pacific Railway. Bernie was tended in Washed Port by a sensitive and experienced cat lover who sent weekly reports of his progress to us out West.

The tragedy struck after we returned. I had always felt Bernie had difficulty seeing, and one day when I returned home from work, I was greeted by an alarmed ex-husband.

"What happened?"

"It's Bernie."

"Where is he?"

"He's . . . he's there on the lawn."

"Well, what happened?"

"I found Bernie in the street; looks like he was hit by a car."

I looked over at a cardboard box that had been flattened out and was covered with blood. Bernie seemed to be asleep.

I screamed. The numbing shock that something had happened to Bernie gave me a frozen feeling.

When I realized that Bernie was dead, I said, "Please get the body out of here—Jonah will crack up when he sees it."

My almost-ex refused to do anything. "He'll think I did away with Bernie. I don't want to take the rap."

"Well, Jonah will think he ran away. Why does he have to see a cat corpse?"

I was still feeling cold chills running through my body. That cat reminded me of myself when I got knocked down by my husband in one of his instant temper tantrums. The rage exploded inside me. "You bastard—worried about taking the rap for a cat death—you never thought about the rap for wife-beating . . . almost leaving your children motherless."

Now I was foaming at the mouth and couldn't speak. I just went up to my room and waited for the worst.

The worst happened pretty soon when Jonah came screaming into the house.

"Bernie—Bernie's . . . dead! . . ."

"I know."

There were tears in his eyes and in mine.

"I loved Bernie. He was a beautiful person . . . cat . . . human being."

"I know, Jonah," I said.

Keith his older brother slammed into the house after school.

"Jonah, did you see it?"

Jonah couldn't speak. He just cried and cried and cried.

I couldn't speak.

My almost-ex had left like a rat deserting a sinking ship which was his usual response. I just sat numbly in the chair.

After a while I heard Keith say, "Jonah, you have to realize that life is that way—you just can't take things for granted. Nothing lasts forever."

Jonah was dissolving into hysterical weeping. Keith said, "Pull yourself together. You have to," but Jonah blubbered on completely hysterical. Finally, Keith began to cry also. The two of them sobbed for two days.

They ate nothing. On the morning of the third day, they decided to bury Bernie. They found an old shovel and dug a grave near the garage about one third of an acre behind the house. They made a tombstone that said: "To Bernie whom we'll always love" and they went outside in the crisp, morning air to pay their last respects.

By this time they had acquired a little black and white kitten who witnessed the funeral with them, and scampered about in the yard. I watched them all from the bedroom window, hoping that Jonah would recover from his deep sorrow. They allowed no one else to attend the funeral, and they were out in the yard reciting Kaddish in Hebrew over the grave for Bernie's lost soul. It wasn't until they came inside after the burial that they finally accepted food. It had been three days since they had eaten anything.

Jonah sat in the living room hugging the little kitten and saying over and over, "Bernie was the most human cat in the world. He loved people. He would sit next to me and understand how I felt."

Both boys nodded. "Jonah, you have to get over this. You can't let it ruin your life," said Keith.

"But, Bernie is gone . . . he'll never snuggle up to me again . . ."

Keith calmed Jonah down, and they decided to get another cat to replace Bernie. Soon they were leaving notices at the supermarket.

"Wanted—a kitten. Call 959-0991."

After a few days a man in town offered what he referred to as his 'kitten.' Jonah was overjoyed as he and Keith went to pick up the kitten. But when they got home this animal looked at least three years old. It seemed this so-called kitten was schizoid. He hid under the furniture and only came out to eat at night after we went to sleep. When he banged around the room at night he knocked the place to pieces. In the daylight, he hid.

The little black and white kitten who had followed Jonah around belonged to a family across the street who retrieved him after several days when they thought he'd gone missing. Jonah had been feeding the neighbor's little kitten and realized that he had to go home when the owners came looking for him.

In the meantime, after several weeks of trying to coax this fifteen-pound crazy cat from under the couch each day, Jonah finally said to me, "I think I'm going to give this cat back. I want a kitten I can love. I'm not a cat psychiatrist, and I've tried everything and he still hides."

After a few more days of frustration, Jonah finally gave up and called the owner, who agreed to take him back. Now the search began for another kitten. At last Jonah found a little kitten, who arrived on our doorstep and fell madly in love with "Weiner," Jonah's other cat.

Before we knew enough to control their passions, she was the proud mother of two kittens and Weiner was a father. Jonah was overjoyed for now he had four furry friends, and he could forget Bernie. At the back of his mind there was always his deep sense of loss over Bernie. But the kittens who were born behind the couch spent their first three weeks in the linen closet where the mother cat hid them.

Jonah was the only human the mother cat allowed near her kittens. Things were fine until a few months later Jonah discovered that the mother cat was pregnant again. He already had four mouths to feed, and it was with alarm that he viewed the next delivery.

"We've got to fix the mother cat," he said. "We're going to have too many kittens."

"Well, if the operation costs too much, it could be a problem," I said. Finally, after some intense searching, we located a vet we could afford who still charged 1940 prices. Jonah was given instructions on what to do after this next pregnancy. The cat delivered five more kittens and now Jonah had nine cats and kittens. This time he was getting worried and lately, I hadn't heard Bernie mentioned.

The vet's instructions were to remove the mother cat right after the nursing period and to bring her to the animal hospital. The mother cat was fixed, and Jonah breathed a sigh of relief. Except for the fact that he still had nine cats, he was happy. He scoured the neighborhood for cat lovers. He offered food and care to anyone who would take some kittens. The signs went up at the supermarket again. It was a long, hard fight to get families to take some of the kittens.

Jonah badgered everyone in sight on his newspaper route. Finally, he engineered four adoptions—a minor miracle. All during this period, the mother cat was recuperating.

But after several weeks something strange happened to her. She was running around the house with a long white "something" hanging from her rear end, leaving a trail of mess behind her. I was afraid the operation hadn't taken and a piece of her intestine was trailing behind her. Jonah called every vet in the entire county for advice. Finally one of the doctors said he thought the cat had swallowed a string. Jonah was told to snip it off at the end and give the cat castor oil.

This vet had returned the call at about midnight, and suddenly Jonah and Keith stormed into my room looking for rubber gloves and scissors.

I heard Keith say, "Jonah, keep calm, aren't I always good in a crisis?"

Jonah nodded.

I gave them disposable plastic gloves and a pair of scissors. They marched out at midnight looking like two surgeons ready to enter an amphitheatre. The cat had been confined to the screened-in porch by now because she was messing up the whole house and running around wildly and in great discomfort.

As they ran downstairs to attend to the cat, I heard the front door slam and cracked up laughing. When they came inside a few minutes later they had a foot of string in their gloved hands and the cat had calmed down.

The next morning I had castor oil on my shopping list.

Chapter 38

MY OFFICE, SCENE OF MASS MADNESS

My office is still another scene of mass madness. It is in the quiet confines of my little stall that I write, confer and try to keep the lid from blowing off. Remember, I always keep SMILING, even if it kills me.

The best description of my office that can be given is the one an artist gave me after her first two-hour visit. "I had to go home and sleep for four hours after being in your office. How do you stand that, every day?"

My answer was, "But you were there on a slow day."

Actually the world would consider me a totally liberated woman if they looked closely at my life at the office. I have a male secretary (an aspiring young actor, and he has an assistant, an aspiring playwright, male, also). Now, when I was growing up if anyone had told me I was going to have two male secretaries, five cats, a huge house and a miniscule bank account with two sons in Ivy League colleges and one almost-ex-husband when I hit perimenopause I wouldn't have believed it. But, as they say, 'truth is stranger than fiction' and in my case, my daily life upholds this concept.

The irony of my daily life was that the totally unexpected seemed to be happening all the time. The official reason I was given one of the male secretaries was because my boss told me there were no more secretaries who could keep up with the pace of my work. The young, female secretaries kept requesting a transfer or quitting altogether.

I was shocked when he said, "You can only have Gerard, and he's slow!"

Well, it's true Gerard started typing slowly, but he definitely wasn't slow in the head, having received a Fulbright in Drama at Oxford University along with a few other credentials he didn't want anyone to find out about.

When he told me these things about himself, he said, "Please don't tell anyone here, or I'll be fired because I'm overqualified as a secretary, and I have to earn bread to continue my acting lessons."

I was sworn to secrecy.

Of course, Gerard had a few other problems, like the fact that he wanted to see a psychiatrist because he wasn't happy about his sex life. When he started showing up in the morning looking like he was stoned I asked him what was going on.

"I've taken a job from ten p.m. to four a.m. at a gay bar in order to pay my psychiatrist," he answered.

After a few days of this, Gerard looked like a sepulcher.

"Gerard, tell your damned psychiatrist to cut your fee or he'll have a dead patient. Then he won't get any fee at all."

Gerard looked at me. "After all, Gerard, he doesn't have to earn $400,000 a year. He can live just as well on $390,000."

Gerard had to quit the night job. Even though he had gotten the psychiatrist to cut his fee, he was spacing out from lack of sleep. He also told me, however, that he had gone cold turkey, going off Dexedrine, which some doctor had given him seven years before and to which he had become addicted. After a few days of bizarre behavior, Gerard was trying to work with the shakes and was shouting at one and all, including the top executives in the building. When one of the execs called me into his office gasping and choking one afternoon, I figured Gerard's days were numbered.

"That, that secretary of yours, I'm going to kick him out of here—do you know what he . . . said?"

"Please, calm down. What did Gerard do now?"

"I'm not holding Gerard against you, I'll get you another secretary—believe me."

"Please, please calm down . . . I do believe you . . . I do."

He was so upset he couldn't tell me what had happened. One of the secretaries did tell me and she reported that Gerard had shouted at this top honcho and insulted him. I knew Gerard was the son of a four-star general and a mother who had dressed him in girl's clothes until he was six years old. Wanting to be an actor was not in his father's field of vision as an occupation for his son and Gerard thought his mother was crazy to have dressed him as a girl when he was young. The arts were Gerard's last refuge and Shakespeare and Oxford University beckoned to him. However, getting an acting job in New York had so far eluded him and so he ended up as my secretary for the time being.

Having turned into a management consultant/ psychiatric social worker at the office and a wild-eyed financier at home, there were times when I wondered where it would all lead. There were days when I thought of the pastoral moments of my youth when I had small babies and all I had to worry about was whether or not they got scraped on the knee, had a fever or got hit by a swing in the playground.

All these past moments are forgotten in the rush of the present with new memories rushing by so fast. I do like to accomplish things quickly and in a way, Gerard often slowed things down. But he was funny. One day he told an ardent Catholic staff member that he agreed with her, "A good man is hard to find." I thought she was going to pass out. Gerard had a way of advertising his life style, leaving very little to the imagination.

I <u>have</u> had to put a stop to his phone calls. I couldn't handle all his suitors. He had more than I did and that was cause for alarm.

Chapter 39

THE HIMALAYAS AND WHY MERV
CANCELLED THE SHERPAS

In order to swallow the bitter pills of reality, I've taken up with another man. A psychic healer. The reason for this should be fairly apparent from the pages of this book. However, in my search for peace and security, I will try just about anything. Since all traditional routes have failed, mysticism was the only route left.

Whatever it is, I have become a believer. The world had turned into so many banalities that I would do anything to remain SANE. At all costs, I do not intend to be driven to a nervous breakdown by five cats, two teenage sons, a broken car, refrigerator, dishwasher, furnace and freezer, one leaking roof, a front lawn that my neighbors are ashamed of, a peeling house (because it hasn't been painted since we moved in twelve years ago), a bank account that disappears before I put money into it, the LIRR, my middle-age menopausal crisis, neighbors, the depression (yes, not recession), my son's college tuition, doctor's, lawyer's and accountant's bills, not to mention dentist's, food bills and my job.

All these aforementioned items are usually juggled on my way to New York on the LIRR, or on the New York City subway system, because if you are too busy to think, most of your problems will change by next week. The broken freezer will become a broken hot water heater, the furnace will find still another way not to heat the house even if I spend four thousand dollars to fix it and to fill the oil tank.

There are days when I am ready to become a priest, join a merchant ship and go around the world like Joseph Conrad, or else escape to parts unknown—deepest Africa, Tierra del Fuego, the outback of Australia, New Zealand, the virgin territory of British Columbia, the wilds of Alaska, Hawaii, the Bahamas, Paris, London and Milano, Austria and Geneva, Copenhagen and Leningrad. My mind reads like the photocopy of a travelogue.

Each day I'm somewhere else. One day I'm going to chuck the LIRR, find a new lifestyle and run off to Tahiti with a lover. These fantasies occur regularly and overwhelm my psyche. They derive from the heavy strain of working to support a family. Most men share them with me.

My friend Mervyn was going to climb the Himalayas. Mervyn, a peaceful New Jersey suburbanite, as he explained was seeking peace and tranquility in esoteric Eastern doctrines in order to free his inner being. Mervyn is a dear man who has pulled his head together since his business partner went into "male menopause," and started chasing seventeen-year-old girls in open, flowered shirts, wearing love beads and sandals.

Merv, much more staid and sober, chose to find his answers not in sex, but in austere disciplines of the mind and heart. Hence, as Merv described his parents' reaction, in *narrischkeiten*, which in translation means *meschuggeh*, another well-known local word adding up to "foolishness."

Now, Merv has pursued his Eastern esotericism regularly and relentlessly, as I well know because we chased all over Mulberry Street in Greenwich Village for fresh ricotta cheese needed for our "fire diet," which was part of our Arica Training. It was at Arica that I met Merv and his description of hiring Sherpas to help him climb the Himalayas was a riot. Of course, with everything ready to go, getting out of his Toyota wagon one day, his knee gave out and he had to cancel the trip, Sherpas and all!

This of course relieved his ninety-five-year-old mother of an incipient heart attack and stroke as she groaned, "Thank God," when Merv hurt his knee.

Merv's wife, however, had booked a European trip when she heard he would be gone five weeks in the wilds of the East, and she left on her trip while Merv had to cancel. He spent those five weeks seeking solace from his local rabbi because, as he said, "Don't think I was horny just because my wife was away." When she returned the homecoming must have been something to behold.

Now, everyone in this esoteric group has cleaned their "karma" but I, who haven't got the extra dollars, have not. I do not know what "dirty karma" means in the ultimate scheme of things, but if I could afford the fifteen hundred bucks I would definitely "clean my karma" immediately.

When I think back to the stages of my bad marriage it was definitely "dirty karma" all the way. What I want is a second chance at "cleaning up my karma," but right now I can't afford it because it's winter and that means I have too many bills to pay. In winter, I have much less money than in the summer because oil bills burn up my entire salary.

That reminds me of the day I met a prominent Arab spokesman for peace in the Middle East who wanted to discuss the issues. I was going to ask him to pay my heating bill in the winter. I was at a meeting with a friend trying to work for world peace, which is what I do when I am not working at cleaning up my own karma.

Now that is a paradox. World peace will have to come about by miraculous conception because most of the peace groups in this country hate each other. This is a cause for concern and a problem—if you can't get the peace groups to stop fighting, forget about the world. Either that or the peace people are really not very "peaceful people" themselves.

All this exhausts me in the light of what has to be done in this world. There is karma to clean, peace to keep, environments to preserve, pollution to overcome, depression to avert, and in between what's left but sports, teenage problems, aging, unwed motherhood, the high divorce rate and inflation. Now, if all these issues can generate more than superficial solutions, I will go to bed at night with a sense of serenity.

Which brings me back to the beginning of this chapter and my fantasies. It is because I know that these pressures will not stop that I see myself jetting off to Geneva, Paris and the Australian outback. I am determined to escape the lifestyle I have been following. I wonder if working women have the same rate of coronary failure men do. So why hustle when Micronesia has coral reefs to swim in and coconuts to pick?

Chapter 40

THE BAR MITZVAH

When I returned home from Janice it was because my youngest son asked me to come home.

"Janice, I can't stay away forever. I have to go back to my children."

"Get them and go away."

"I want to, but right now that would disrupt their lives totally. I have to get him to accept a divorce."

"You may not live to get out."

"I know, but I have to get back now and see what I can do."

It was two months until my youngest son's thirteenth birthday, the traditional Bar Mitzvah. I had scrimped and saved to have one for him. It would be inexpensive, but I would manage. My husband tried to steal the money from me.

"I need the money!" he screamed. "What does he need to be confirmed for? I am in financial trouble," he continued, screaming.

I knew at that moment that I would get my divorce, no matter what happened. I came home with plans to get out. I needed to run the Bar Mitzvah and right after that I would serve the divorce papers. The lawyer told me not to be anywhere around him when those papers were served. We planned for them to be served right after the Bar Mitzvah.

It was sad to split up a family. But this marriage had collapsed long ago like a house of cards. The Bar Mitzvah was held at our house a few weeks after I returned home from staying with Janice. It was a nightmare to encounter him.

I didn't know what to do. I wanted to flee, but the lawyer said to go back home, or I could be charged with abandonment. This was to be the last battle before total warfare broke out.

The day of the Bar Mitzvah arrived. It was a sunny spring day at the end of March. It was held in the garden. At the synagogue, earlier in the day, many relatives filed in to hear my son read from the Torah. This little young man was well versed in Hebrew having spent his elementary school years in a Yeshiva. He sang the tones beautifully.

I watched my mother weeping. The march with the Torah held high was an inspiration. In the darkness of my life the tears sparkled down my cheeks and against the heaviness of my heart was this space for the grace of God.

The men of the congregation danced with the Torah and my son led them. His father, never having been Bar Mitzvah'd, could not participate. My husband stood there silently watching, never having learned the values of a life worth living. I prayed my sons would have the strength to surmount their troubles and be the young men they were truly born to be.

After the services all our relatives and friends came home with us for the celebration. The musicians played folk music, the food was served, and there was laughter and joy in the house. Everyone was celebrating the ascent into manhood by one young boy welcomed by the men of the congregation into the responsibilities and opportunities of manhood. It is interesting that my husband had never been Bar Mitzvah'd. He was considered too sophisticated for such a tribal ritual.

To undiscerning eyes, this party would have looked like a normal family party. My parents, my sons, Janice, Carol, my husband's mother and the family doctor who had all shared my grief—they all knew this celebration was a time bomb ticking away before the dissolution of my family.

The music floated through the house. What a place of joy this big old house could have been. The gardens sprinkled with purple and yellow flowers looked like a rainbow in the sunlight. Assorted children of all ages scampered about. Two young men from the Merchant Marine Academy served drinks to the guests, and a young woman from a nearby college served the food. Everyone enjoyed the party. I sensed a dream of the future for my sons, and prayed silently to be able to lift them from this terrible life they had lived to a grander place. A place where they could know love and peace and joy once more.

I knew the time bomb was ticking inside, but outside I faced the world well dressed, well coiffed and smiling all the way. Just another happy American family down the block.

Chapter 41

SEPARATION AGREEMENT

When I thought back to the past, I felt as if I were at the bottom of a deep well trying to climb up to the light. This divorce and separation experience had become surreal. Chipping away at twenty years of intimacy and the gradual dissolution of close family bonds was still painful.

I suddenly woke up to find that past patterns were dissolving, new experiences became another way of life. Family bonds shaken by divorce were like the boughs of a tree that can be broken by very strong winds. I don't think anyone should minimize the terrible pain of separation brought about by breaking up a long marriage. People joke about divorcees, but it might be more fitting if they treated the two people involved as if they had just experienced the death of a close relative. The period of mourning for lost love, unrequited dreams and broken intimacy was long and painful for me.

Now I am numbed by the thought of closeness. I know healing will take place ultimately, but this process is agonizing. I find attachments hard to break.

The shock of how deeply I reacted to the final separation came when the summer after three-and-one-half years of haggling and wrangling I finally saw a set of papers called SEPARATION AGREEMENT!

I thought I was pretty cool having waited three-and-one-half years for them. I was past caring. The papers were anti-climactic. I had long since given up believing I would live to see the day they were signed. These weren't signed. They were just a draft of the agreement. My head felt fuzzy. I wasn't very good at reading legal briefs. I conferred with three lawyers, all relatives and friends, also my parents, my brother and God.

The words were like so many worms crawling along the pages. I was sure I understood what they said, but I still couldn't figure out if my husband in his usual "I'm gonna get you" style had actually screwed me or not. I knew he was out to make things as unbearable as possible and he had already succeeded for many years. All I really wanted was his signature to freedom because lawyers had long since warned me that anything he put on paper wasn't worth the paper it was written on.

So I figured I was ahead if he agreed to do anything at all. I was shocked to see that he agreed to do more than I ever expected. You see, he had written the document himself because he insisted that we couldn't afford the legal fees.

He even put in alimony if I was sick or unemployed. After twenty years, he would give me a hundred dollars a month to feed myself if I couldn't do it or so it said on paper.

I thought I was feeling pretty cool when it struck. Gerard, my secretary, walked up to me on a hot, August afternoon, the day after I saw the papers and said, "You look white as a ghost—is anything wrong?"

"I don't think so," I said.

I knew I had had an unusually long period the month before; for some reason things were out of whack with my body. I attributed it to a long walk in the hot July sun. For some reason, that menstrual period just went on and on for three weeks. My regular doctor said not to worry, and I couldn't get an appointment with the gynecologist until mid-September.

I was pretty upset because I could have bled to death by the time he could see me. In exasperation, I called another doctor and he agreed to see me immediately. He took all the tests and said he would let me know. Just as I was leaving, he said, "Are you under any unusual stress these days?"

I said, "No. I'm just getting legally separated from my husband, that's all."

"Ah-hah," he said.

"Ah-hah, what?"

"That could do it."

"Do what?"

"Disrupt your menstrual cycle. You know you're too young for menopause."

"I may be too young, Doc, but I wouldn't mind a little menopause. I've had it with being a woman for a while."

"Don't worry," he said, "your body will adjust. I don't think it's serious, and I'll let you know when the results of the tests come in."

"Thanks," I shrugged and left.

That was in July, and I had forgotten that at the end of August I was due for another period.

Gerard kept looking at me.

"You don't look good. Why don't you go home?" he said.

"I'm fine," I replied.

As I got up from the chair, I saw a pool of blood. Now that had never happened to me before. I had been wearing precautionary protection because of what had happened in July, but when I saw the blood, I sat right down in the chair. The gal I was working with looked over at me with a knowing smile. Gerard had left the room closing the conference door behind him.

"Listen," I said, "I can't get up." I felt about to faint.

"How old are you?" she asked.

"Forty."

"You have all the signs of menopause. I bled all one summer when I was forty-three and never had another period again."

"But the doctor said I'm too young."

"What does he know? He's only a man!" she said.

What she didn't know about was my impending divorce. That is because I was very close-mouthed about my private life at the office. Also, I wanted to forget my rotten, private life, so I left it back in Great Neck before I went to work in the morning. And a relief it was, too.

By now she had convinced me that this would be my last period ever, and I was ready to do a buck-and-wing. When I stood up, I fainted.

My friend Gena was called in. As the veteran of two marriages and the hysterectomy war with cancer of the uterus at thirty two, she was deemed the most qualified person to pull me together. I'm sure one of the cleaning staff took care of the blood on the chair, but the next thing I knew, Gerard and Gena were literally carrying me and my briefcase to the elevator.

Gena got into the cab with me and put me on the LIRR train telling the conductor to help me off. She shoved several dollars at me, telling me to take a cab at the other end and yelling, "CALL THE DOCTOR," as the train pulled out of the station.

When I got home and into bed I called Gerard. "The deadline—we have a 500-page book to get to press next week!"

Gerard said, "Leave it to me, I know what to do. Get into bed and stay there; you've been working too hard. Listen, maybe you need a D and C. My mother had one when she was going through menopause."

"Gerard," I shouted, "I'm alright. I just haven't had a vacation in a year and a half."

"Stay in bed," he said. "I'll take care of everything."

"Thanks, Gerard," I said, and I hung up and practically fainted. I felt like a huge gush of blood had left my groin, and I was afraid to move.

Now panic began to set in. I was all alone in my house, except for the cats, and they don't speak English. I was very weak and frightened.

"What if I do need a D and C?" I thought. "I can't—it dawned on me I had no medical insurance coverage for surgery. I became hysterical. My husband and I were separating and he had refused to include me in his coverage. So I had just sent in for a new policy for myself, but it was too late if I were going to the hospital very soon.

I fell back on the pillow. The precious money I had saved for my son's college tuition was going to have to pay for the surgeon. I was hysterical, I couldn't go on. I, who never think of suicide, was ready to think of it. My frustration reached such an abyss of doom that I wanted to give up. Damned world—damned divorce—DAMN EVERYTHING!

I lay there in a stupor of agony and helplessness like a skinned rabbit. There was no one I could ask for help. In my pain I reached for the phone and called San Francisco. My parents listened to my tale of woe and said, "Why don't you take your children and come out West. At least college here is free . . ."

It sounded like a great idea. Anything far away from my life at the moment. My mother reassured me that she would soon be flying to New York to visit, and as soon as she got here, everything would be fine. My mother's faith in her own omnipotence was astounding and I almost believed her. Until I hung up the phone and felt another gush of blood. I was certain that I was bleeding to death and would never live to see my mother fly across the country. My hours were numbered.

This time I reached for the phone and called the doctor.

"How are you, Ms. G.?" he said, "I was just going to call you, the tests all came back. You are fit as a fiddle."

"Then why am I bleeding to death?" I asked poignantly.

"Bleeding to death—you mean you have a heavy menstrual flow."

"I guess you could call it that. I thought it was a hemorrhage myself."

"Now, now, relax—this happens to women every day."

"But not to me. What do I do now?"

"Just stay in bed. First get some ice cubes and place them on your stomach every hour for about twenty minutes. Then call me tomorrow morning."

"O.K." I said, but I was sure I would bleed to death before then.

I staggered downstairs to the refrigerator which looked like it was about to conk out in the August heat wave. I retrieved some ice cubes and staggered back upstairs, punchy and thinking that if another appliance went on the blink, I would have to go on welfare. (Little did I know at the time that my furnace was about to die just before the cold weather.) I hadn't really tuned into the fact that it was leaking 15 buckets of water a day from the water gauge. But at the moment I was in such bad shape myself I had all I could do to live until morning.

Gena called me to find out how I was.

"I'm dying."

"I told you to take your damned vacation!" she screamed. "You don't take care of your body and now it's telling you something."

"It sure is."

"Listen, when I had cancer, I hadn't been to the doctor for eleven months, that's all. If I had come in for my six-month check-up they would have caught me in time."

"But Gena, the doctor said the Pap test was fine. I don't have cancer," I shouted back at her.

"My Pap test didn't show it the first time either. You have got to take care of your body. It's the only one you have."

"I know, I know—I am, I am," I yelled. "I'm in bed—resting." I almost screamed. "Resting!"

"Stay there!" she yelled and hung up.

There wasn't much I could do but stay in bed, and I was running out of sanitary napkins. I had run through the last ten I had in the last three hours. I called the drug store to ask them to deliver some.

The conversation got a little hairy. "Could you leave them at my door? I can't walk downstairs, I'm ill."

"Sure, but you have to give us a check—we will only make deliveries to you C.O.D."

"But I'm sick, I can't go downstairs again. Couldn't you trust me until I can get someone to take the check to you?"

"No, Mrs. G, the last time we trusted your family your husband ran up a bill for three years and we had to sue him for the money."

"But I—we . . ." I hung up.

What difference did it make anyway, I wasn't going to live until the morning. I lay there about to die. Jonah came running in from school and dashed up the stairs.

I called weakly, "Jonah . . ."

He came into the darkened room.

"I'm sick, Jonah, quite sick."

"Ugh," he said. "What's wrong?"

"I'm bleeding a lot."

He didn't really know what to say.

"I think I'm going to feed the cats now," he said backing out of the door, acting a little embarrassed at my women's troubles.

My almost-ex-husband called and said, "Did you read the agreement?"

"What agreement? Oh . . . that one."

"Yeah—what did you think of it?"

"To tell you the truth, I'm dying—so I can't comment on the agreement. And if you happen by this house in the next day or so bring super giant sanitary napkins because I'm bleeding to death, and I can't get any credit at the drug store."

I hung up, but as I did I heard him say, "You'll have to reimburse me. I don't have the money."

"You bastard!" I shouted at the dial tone.

The ice began to ease my pain and slow the bleeding.

But every time I went to the bathroom, the toilet looked like a pool of bright, red blood. I staggered back into bed. All night, I was sure it was my last night on earth. By now I felt anxious and so weak that I couldn't think.

When morning finally came, I grabbed the phone.

"Doctor Z—it's Mrs. G."

"Well, you didn't die, did you?" he said.

"I'm still bleeding and I can't go to work."

"Calm down, you can't go to work—so what."

"I have to support my family. I can't stay home."

"You're sick."

Anyway, I reported to him that I was still bleeding now for what had been four days non-stop and now on the fourth day he finally decided that it <u>was</u> a hemorrhage after all.

"Why didn't you realize it before?"

"Because we have to let nature take its course. Besides I'm convinced it's emotional. I could find nothing physically wrong with you. You're just reacting to your divorce."

"I want the divorce, I want it!" I shouted.

"But your body doesn't. You have to adjust to these shocks gradually."

"My marriage was a shock . . ." I shouted, "my divorce is a liberation."

"Now, calm down, give me the name and phone number of your druggist, and I'll phone this prescription to him and have him deliver it."

I gave him the druggist's number and shouted into the phone, "Tell him someone will pick it up and will bring a check—don't ask him to deliver it."

As I hung up, I heard the doctor say, "And call me tomorrow and let me know how the pills work."

I lay back exhausted and weak and fell asleep praying for some respite from this life.

Chapter 42

BIZ TRIP: TAKE PILLS, EAT LIVER

God must have answered my prayers because the pills stopped the bleeding and I was back at work a week later. Of course, I was eating liver three times a day and trying to keep my head together, and if my friend Nella had not brought a check to the drug store for the pills, I might not have recovered. I owed her my life. She also brought me a huge container of buttered popcorn to cheer me up, which it did because I really hadn't eaten much in the last four days. Bless her!

In the midst of all this, my office was turning into an obstetric ward. Between my hemorrhages there were also five pregnant females in all stages of gestation, three of whom were delivering momentarily. I prayed hourly that I had just experienced my final menstrual period and was about to enter menopause. I couldn't afford to get sick next month because I was scheduled for a business trip, and I couldn't get out of it.

When I approached my boss asking for mercy, she said hysterically, "You have to go. Take pills, eat liver, call your doctor."

That's exactly what I did.

When I went to see him for a check-up, he said, "You're fine. I told you it was the divorce."

"But next month, what if I hemorrhage in another state?"

He laughed. "What makes you think they don't have gynecologists in Pennsylvania?"

"I know they do, but I don't know them."

He smiled. "Take your pills along, and at the first sign of bleeding, start taking them. The worst is over."

"I hope so," I said as I walked out of his office.

When it was time to go on my business trip, I had already spent the previous three weeks visiting the local Christian Science church and reading everything in sight that Mary Baker Eddy had written. I had to stay well. I had to heal myself. I couldn't afford this disease business because I was supporting two sons, five cats and a big, white elephant house built in the 1890s during the gas light era. After all, how many religions can you name that were founded by a woman? And even if I was born a Chassidic Jew I needed to be healed and I would take whatever help I could get, wherever I could find it.

I was sure I would never survive this business trip after the *Walpurgisnacht* of my last period. However, the woman who went with me had been through the same thing and she reassured me that in the event of any trouble, she would deliver me to the nearest hospital, rapidly. I wondered if Blue Cross crosses state lines, but mostly I was sure I'd never make it back from this trip.

Gena didn't help.

"Tell them you can't go. You've got to take care of your body. Stand up for your rights."

I didn't and I went.

Gena stood up for her rights, and soon got fired. But she had more money than I, and her current pressures were not as extreme.

Chapter 43

FAMILY COURT COUNSELING

No one would believe that I was chased by this raving maniac and hiding in a room in the Family Court building. But, that's exactly what happened. He blew up at a session of family counseling which he had requested himself. He said he wanted to save our marriage. The family counselor, an ex-minister, was a very gentle, kindly man who had left the ministry to help unhappy couples.

I knew I wanted out of this marriage and made it very clear at a visit with the lawyers when we met one evening. He called me at the university where I worked and pleaded for us to make one last try to SAVE OUR MARRIAGE. Would I not, at least, show up at the family court? I didn't want to, but I did want to appear reasonable. I had long since given up any hope of saving this marriage. It was ridiculous, but I said O.K. to seem reasonable.

He said that he had set up an appointment and that they were very hard to get. I showed up at these appointments. By now he was living with his mother in New York City and the only time I saw him was once a week in the counselor's office at the Family Court building. And that was a trial.

The counselor was a very patient person. My almost-ex was always ready to jump at the slightest word, thought or deed that appeared to impinge on his own point of view which is that I was wrong and totally the cause of all our marital woes. Still sore and hurting inside from all the years of abuse and battering, I really didn't want to be there and listen to his lies making himself the victim.

After a series of these sessions, he finally blew up violently at one of them. It was hard for him to go for too long without getting his buttons pushed. He started chasing me. I was so tuned into my terror that I ran out of the counseling room in an instant. I prayed for the marriage counselor to pacify him. I had run out and hidden in a small kitchen nearby, shutting the door behind me. I whispered to the night guard and asked him to please watch out for me.

Shaking all over, I realized that even in the Family Court building this bastard was still trying to get me. This was insane. The whole scene was mad. I shivered in fear of this Vesuvian eruption, and kept praying and shaking, praying and shaking.

I looked around in the little kitchen I was hiding in and saw a set of knives on the wall. My terror escalated. I heard him running around outside, ranting and screaming, "I'll get you . . . I'll get you!"

I couldn't stop shaking. Every organ inside my body felt like jelly . . . it quaked and shook. The terror escalated when I heard his voice nearby. Then the counselor urged him back into his office. I didn't know how I would get back home and I was quaking with terror. When I heard the door close to the counselor's office, I asked the guard to see to it that my almost-ex left before the counselor got me out of my hiding place. I went back into hiding. I felt a cold sweat break out all over my body and the minutes seemed like hours. Finally, Don, the counselor, got me out of the little kitchen where I was hiding.

"Come into my office," he said, "He's gone."

I was still afraid to come out.

"I'll tell you what," said the tall, slender minister. "Let's get into my car and I'll take you home. We can talk on the way."

"O.K.", I said.

The guard and the counselor walked me to the car and we got in. The guard went back into the building. Driving along the highway, I was still shaking.

The grey-haired ex-minister was a gentle, tender man and I felt safe with him. I was so afraid my almost-ex would be at the house when I arrived that I felt the terror escalating on the way as we talked.

"I don't often recommend divorce," he said. "My job is to save marriages. But in this case, there is no way out. None. You have to get free of this. You don't deserve this. You are still young. Get a divorce!"

"That's what I am trying to do. But he's unwilling to sign any agreement. He's totally bananas."

"I will counsel him into divorce for his own sake. Maybe he can still salvage his own life after this."

"I sure hope so," I said. "Because the way he is going now, he's wrecking everyone else's life and certainly his own."

I silently prayed again for salvation.

As we drove along in his green car, I prayed that one day I would meet a gentle, kind man like this man, and for once feel safe in the world—something I hadn't felt in many years.

When he dropped me at my house, he said, "Now call the police and ask for protection. Refer them to me if they give you any trouble. Here's my card, and here's my home phone number if you need it."

I climbed out of his car and was shaking all over again. The house looked big and like a dark monster against the night sky. All the shadows of the trees and bushes might be hiding this maniac. I was still quaking with fear when I opened the door and went inside.

Don waited until I was inside the house before driving off. I was still quaking with fear as I opened the door and ran up the stairs and barricaded the door of my bedroom. I heard my children call to me.

"Are you home, mom?"

"Yes."

They went back into their bedrooms to watch TV.

I dialed the police.

This was not the first time I had called for help. They said, O.K., they would patrol the house, but to be sure to call if I heard any sounds in the night. They told me they would arrive immediately.

I lay down on the bed in total exhaustion. I needed to sleep because I had to wake up at 6:00 a.m. get to work. I lay there in terror wondering when all this would end. How much more could I endure?

I fell asleep in utter exhaustion and terror. Every time a sound echoed in the night, I jumped and reached for the phone near my bed. My heart thumped wildly and at each sound, I jumped and then I tried to calm down and get to the morning. Finally, I fell asleep and when the light filtered into the windows in the morning, I looked around the room. The sunlight beamed through the red curtains, the morning had come and I was still alive. I was still alive.

Chapter 44

PRAYING FOR DELIVERANCE

My life continued on like this for several years. I sought all sorts of help . . . and when things cooled down I went home to my children. Some of this time I was in graduate school and trying to escape by getting enough education to earn a living as a teacher. My mind was plundered and pummeled in this war, but I kept on studying. I kept on concentrating. I disciplined myself and told myself I would be leaving soon, as soon as I got my master's degree as a teacher.

Sometimes in the summer months when I had to run away, I would hide in my own garden, sleeping in the bushes next to the earth. Exhausted and frightened, I tried to stay awake and alert. But finally, I would fall asleep hiding behind a bush—always praying for deliverance.

I kept on going. I knew there had to be a way out. His sexual behavior was a nightmare. Every time he wanted me, I wanted to run away and finally, I did.

Many times he threw me across the room and punched my breasts until they ached, and then finally he would rape me. I couldn't think farther than the next moment which was to get out of there and run out the door.

This nightmare continued for years and I still don't know why I didn't just run away. I felt such aching responsibility for my children. I planned to finish school and get a job and then take my children out of there. But that was ridiculous. A lot of the time, in the early years, I tried to ignore his insanity, a truly foolish thing to do. When I looked back, there didn't seem to be any sense to my behavior. The truth was that I wasn't strong enough to really end this horror story.

After enough of these incidents had accumulated, I knew that now after my younger son's Bar Mitzvah had taken place this marriage was finally over.

Friends and family had gathered in the garden and the sad, tired eyes of my mother and father had stared back at me. Their only wish was to see this farce, my so called marriage, finally over. I knew this was the last day we were publicly a family. We were a family to the outside world, but in the darkness and the shadows of the house, we were a monstrosity—a lie.

And now looking back at all those years of suffering, I want only to put it all behind me. I am respected in my profession. No one knows of my past life, except for some dear and close friends.

Tomorrow is a breakthrough day. After seven long years of struggling and battling for my freedom, I will finally be divorced. This book is my letter to the world.

Fortunately, I've learned that there is love in the world. From friends, my sons and the cosmos, I am grateful to have lived to share this story and I pray it can help others trapped in the same vicious game I was trapped in for so long.

"There but for the grace of God . . . go I, into the world . . . a free woman."

Chapter 45

NELLA'S HUSBAND PLAYS CUPID

Actually there is no simple answer. Just as I was about to sink into oblivion a male friend decided to rescue me from anomie. Now if I could find a man like Jean Paul Sartre I would be fine. Since there are only a few like him on this planet, I cannot say that my woman's liberationist philosophy is not going to break down in the face of overwhelming odds. I realize Simone de Beauvoir has had much more support for her identity than I because I cannot see Jean Paul tearing up her writing as my husband did mine. (Unless he felt he was sparing the world literary devastation by exercising his best critical judgment.)

The struggle to survive my mental and physical distress has prompted all kinds of emergency measures—vitamins, herb teas, brewer's yeast, yoga, deep breathing exercises, prayer, psychic healers, transcendental meditation and a gamut of psychotherapies that should have cured me of every mental illness known to the Western world. But it has not!

I am still fighting my counter-culture battle which is fast threatening to become WWIII. With such devastation at my mental doorstep, the only solution for my liberated soul is a new husband, a commodity harder to come by than uranium on East Fifty-seventh Street.

So after being rescued by a friend and introduced to a man I'm going to call Goldfinger, I decided to put off my nervous breakdown until after New Year's Eve since I was <u>going out.</u>

Now, to an ordinary person one party invitation may be nothing, but to a divorced woman it is the difference between depression and exaltation. I knew the New Year was going to be a good one when I got on the LIRR to go to the party and the conductor handed me a free ticket and said, "Merry Christmas and Happy New Year!" Such an omen cannot be dismissed lightly, if you know the conductors on the LIRR.

For there are times when they'll practically frisk you if you're standing up with your briefcase in one hand, and books and an overweight pocketbook in the other desperately trying to find your commuter ticket before they put you off the train at the next station.

When I arrived at this happy New Year's party, little did I know what would happen. Innocent that I was, having sworn off men until the movement for women's liberation is permanently entrenched, I was betrayed. Actually, the thinking behind all this was non-existent. I was just reacting out of sheer good humor.

Since my friend's husband decided to play Cupid, he invited a single man I had once met, Rolls Royce and all. Now for someone as poor as I was at the time money had a particular attraction. It was like a set of neon lights blinking in space. Added to the Rolls Royce was an attractive—separated—millionaire.

Now, I am not in the habit of giving up my values for just anyone, but this was different. As it turned out this man decided I should have a tour of his mansion after the New Year, and so I went. It's not every day that I find out how the rich live. Aside from the fact that anyone riding in a Rolls Royce is immediately apparent to every gaping driver on the road, it's a wonder they don't crash into you.

Added to the visit was a blazing fire, soft music and a tour of endless rooms in all states of undress. By that I mean redecoration. This man had found himself spurned by his wife for excessive sex (twice a month), and probably taken to the cleaners for a lot of dough. I had found a fellow sufferer. He, too, was living close to the book *Creative Divorce*, fast replacing the Bible on bedside tables, and he felt the same pain and alienation I had been feeling. Instant rapport!

But, as my mother always said, men and women cannot be friends—because they are different sexes. This very simple statement has shaken the Western World since Helen of Troy and the Eastern World since the Ramayana. The narrow body of knowledge on men and women and love and sex has proliferated into millions of volumes of best sellers and it all boils down to one point. Everyone wants to find somebody to love, and everybody wants to be loved.

As I sat watching the sparks of the fire dwindle, listening to soft music and not having to fight off a lecherous male, I began to relax.

Since every attempt to loosen up your fears and doubts feels like a bout with major surgery, nobody can tell me that love comes easily to people in their forties, fifties and sixties. You are more scared than you ever were and so you put blinkers on your mind and heart. Now, if God could understand that all people need love in abundance from birth to the grave, the world would be a better place!

While going through my middle-age adolescence feeling more pain, grief and sorrow than I care to remember, my two teenage sons are approaching love and life for the first time. I have a feeling it will be easier for them because they are already three steps ahead of me having been born male. I, on the other hand, am struggling to raise my consciousness and to survive with a shred of human dignity and self-respect in a culture that says divorced women are the equivalent of the 'untouchable' class in India. Divorced women are the 'pariah' of our society—to be shunned, feared, hidden, sexually exploited, laughed at and rejected.

The one thing divorced women want is to be accepted and loved, but they are not. The woman who has failed to hold onto her husband's money is now out of the running. She no longer belongs with her married friends. She struggles daily with morbid thoughts (should she take cyanide or sleeping pills?) and she tries to fight a battle against a culture that rejects her.

My own personal challenge consists in trying to find out why it is so difficult to live a human life in an inhuman society. I battle my daily anger by swallowing lots of vitamins and fighting against total abandonment. As I watch alienation, hostility and the lack of love and caring become a way of life for so many women, I wonder if I myself can find happiness one day.

Chapter 46

A PRIEST IN BLUE JEANS

Watching has become one of my central occupations. I try to see what's happening, to gain a perspective, but the world keeps spinning around in odd ways. My life seems to have turned into one long series of projects—my career life, that is. Having been nurtured in the women's liberation movement, I find it hard to return to the old ways. When I think back to years I spent hiding my abilities and fighting for the right to exist as a person, I wonder how I withstood the onslaught of self defeat, but somehow I was always stubborn and didn't want to give in to power or domination.

It is difficult for me to imagine the old programming, though I lived with it for many years. When I see it now it seems archaic, and I wonder how anyone continues to live that way, but some slaves learn to love their chains. Why would I argue with that? It does seem to me that the system has broken down along the way and men are indeed in need of a new set of programs for relationships, not the mindset of the 1940s and 50s.

However, moving from one extreme to another is fraught with difficulty. I keep looking for some solid values, but that too seems to be in flux. I decided that since my romance with the Rolls Royce millionaire had fizzled for the time being what could be more solid than a man of God, a priest?

Now anyone could say that was sound reasoning. Having a few drinks with a priest who happens to look like a movie star is acceptable. But he was having more problems with the opposite sex than I was—if that is at all possible to believe. Since he had decided celibacy was not a healthy way to live, he had brazenly invaded the world of helpless mortals—only to find that was exactly what we were.

I, on the other hand, was ready to take up celibacy after invading the sexploitive singles scene and to run for cover in any monastery or secluded sanctuary I could find. Neither of us had yet found a way. The mass madness that abounds has left me rather quiet as I witness the antics of my fellow sufferers, both male and female. Having discovered that human relationships seem to have a rather high rate of agony attached for those involved, I have decided to play it cool these days and avoid participating.

In my search for an identity, I have called upon God for an answer, since there doesn't seem to be too many answers down here where we, mortals reside. When I look out there at the sordid singles scene called bedroom ping pong, I could throw up. When I look back at my own marriage, I could wretch—so now, the only place to look is up.

Therefore, dating a priest seemed a good place to start. Since the only other priest I had ever known was Father Teilhard de Chardin, the great mystic, this young priest had a hard act to follow. Fortunately, it didn't last too long, and I have now cleaned my karma of one batty ex-husband, one millionaire and one priest. Strangely, I have been gaining detachment from these experiences, for which I am grateful.

Now I'm beginning to wonder if I'm ever going to become attached again because I'm having so much fun watching the passing throng. It's like a parade of characters from the Canterbury Tales. People come and go, I witness their acts and wonder how they see the world. Suddenly everyone is wearing the spectacles of their own mind and seeing the world totally from their own perspective. Sometimes I feel lonely because I seem to be watching a strange set of characters, and often I wonder if I will ever wish to marry again because the world looks so different to me—twenty years later. Perhaps I've gained some perspective from my personal suffering, but there always seems to be a new viewpoint to behold and something new to learn.

I feel calm inside because I feel an inner pull that indicates a growing strength within myself. It is pleasant to experience the world outside, all alone, without clinging to someone else's point of view or being dominated by what someone else perceives the world to be about. The world is made up of many people facing many karmas or kinds of bondage. Some days I look at the world with joy as I begin to find freedom and to accept myself. I know I will never fit the standard package called *Ms. American Female*—but somehow, as I grow through my terrors, fears and conflicts, there seems to be some light at the end of this tunnel.

I am unable to jump into things as so many females I know do. I don't identify being accepted by a man as his sex partner as being the end all of my life. I keep searching for something deeper—wider—higher. Searching for the human element that ties the universe together: elements that a flower, a little child or an old person share. The life force is exciting because it is part of the dream that we will all be loving and caring, that we will move from a society that worships it's genitalia to a society that worships life.

We are at a crossroads. Society can move two ways, it can move into unadulterated selfishness and mass chaos or it can move towards lovingness and serenity and caring. We must make these choices at this time on our planet, and I can't predict where we are going. I can only watch and hope. I see people who are frightened, unloved, desperate, frustrated and evolving. I witness people hurting others and being hurt needlessly. What is the true path of God ? Is it really that we are going to remain less than human or are we going to dare to reach our potential? Are we going to see that to be truly human also implies responsibility towards others?

All this time, for many months, I've wondered how to find peace of mind. I've wondered how I can forget the past. I've wondered how to turn my tears into laughter and how to shed my pain and disillusionment. I want to know how to celebrate the gentle blossoms opening for the first time on a new life, and a new self with the ability to emerge from the frozen ground of a terrible past.

There are no supports when you are groping to find another path. There are only a few friends like flickering candles casting shadows inside a cave. Little lights throwing shadows against the cavernous spaces. You look inside at the darkness, and wonder how you came to be wherever you are, right now. I still continue to search, always wondering where the next space will lead me, where the next path will open. It's like following a moving picture show. The script may have been written and I wonder if I am just reading the lines. Am I just being pulled along a path that destiny has already mapped out for me?

All these thoughts are whirling inside my head, and suddenly I look up at my friend, the priest, who is holding my head in his hands.

"Where am I?" I ask.

"You're alright," he says.

"Alright? What am I doing on the ground?"

"You fainted."

I look around and a crowd has gathered around me. One woman is offering me a paper cup with water in it. There are tears in my eyes.

"But this has never happened to me before. Never."

A policeman and the priest help me up. My head is still sore from having almost hit the ground. The priest had broken my fall with his hand. They took me to the LIRR police station and asked if I wanted to go to the hospital. I said, "No, I probably fainted because I didn't get enough dinner."

That seemed true—so we went to get a hamburger.

As we sat sharing the hamburger, I felt unbelievably cold, as if I was in shock. I couldn't understand what had happened except that earlier I had had an image of a past life in which my friend, the priest, had been a knight. He had come upon me in a forest, and I was dying. My small infant child was there, and he took the child with him and raised him as his son.

As he listened to me, suddenly a tear ran down his cheek. "It feels true," he said, "Because I am getting shivers as you tell me about this scene."

"Of late," he said, "I've wanted to have a son."

But that was all hours before and it seemed so strange that I should have fainted dead away as I was about to board the train for home. I was still shivering in the train station an hour later as we talked. I was so shaken that I was afraid to go home. Finally the time was hitting three a.m. and we decided to stay up till morning because it wasn't very safe to go home so late. I was still feeling chills and was trying to calm down.

My friend had just returned from India and wasn't looking very well, himself. He had had some strange experiences in India, and hadn't fully recovered his own equilibrium. It seemed for him the whole world was churning, and I could feel the energy moving round and round as if he couldn't get hold of himself. We kept on talking until dawn, and the train station began to take on another aspect in the early morning as I watched the regulars come to sleep on the benches. The homeless ones, the wanderers, the seekers, the lost.

I, who had sought shelter in a big, old house with grass and trees around it was suddenly sitting up all night in a train station talking to a priest dressed in blue jeans. The distance traveled in one short year had been very great. It wasn't an angry remark, but I heard him say, "You can choose to protect yourself in those big, suburban houses, but it isn't any kind of protection."

I knew what he said was true. But I was not ready to be as open to the elements as he. But in not protecting himself at all he was suffering the tortures of the damned. He was feeling panic and shock and pain at his own condition, but I didn't know how to help—having barely escaped a skull fracture by the length of a priest's hand.

Chapter 47

BOOK VI CANTO IX OF *THE FAERIE QUEENE*

I always hear with my heart, at first, and I am so gullible that I believe the tales people tell me, but after I take a second look, the tales evaporate, and there lies the truth. We all wish to pursue our fictions for that is an easy way out; then we don't have to face truth. So many women live in fantasy worlds. I really think they believe Prince Charming will come to rescue them. It's a happy fairy tale.

I wonder about all the fairy tales. Is it that we need these fictions to survive? Is reality so numbing with its emptiness that a fairy tale is easier to live with than reality? Somewhere in the dark moments of dreams and memory there may be a fantasy construction mechanism. Maybe this can supply what is missing from reality, especially if reality is too painful to accept. This mythmaking facility of the human organism may actually keep many people alive and functioning. Is it the loss of dreams that would tear people's worlds apart? Every person living deeply in their fantasy worlds will need to reach reality if it challenges their dreams and wakes them up because dreams, often, are not enough.

Sometimes, I wish I had a road map into my internal realities. Then I would seek the signs that point me to the external world. But sometimes everything seems out of reach and I can't get hold of reality. Then I just float through the days waiting for an insight to tie things together.

When I told my friend, a literature professor, about fainting in Penn Station and the strange episode of another lifetime, we were chatting in a local Greek bar near home and drinking retsina wine. The bouzouki music was floating by as she practically shouted:

"That's Book VI Canto IX of the *Faerie Queene*, not a past life!"

"But I never read the *Faerie Queene*. I can't understand Old English, so I've never tried."

She looked at me strangely.

"Well then, maybe it was for real that you tuned into another life. But that scene you described is exactly the central part of the *Faerie Queene*, the most important part of the book."

"Well, that's what happened. And then three hours later, I fainted. I've never fainted before—it was embarrassing."

"Maybe you're onto something."

"What? It's just the same old life. I don't see any great changes, right now, but I can't say my life is dull."

She began quoting from the *Faerie Queene* and it sounded important. It sounded like a clue, so I reminded myself to get the book out of the library. A few days later as I struggled through the Old English, I found the passage she quoted to me:

> "He was to weet by common voice esteemed
> The father of the fayrest *Pastorell*,
> And of her selfe in very deede so deemed;
> Yet was not so, but as old stories tell
> Found her by fortune, which to him befell,
> In th'open fields an Infant left alone,
> And taking vp brought home, and noursed well
> As his owne chyld; for other he had none,
> That she in tract of time accompted was his owne."
>
> *The Faerie Queene* by Edmund Spenser
> 1590

Chapter 48

PAST MEMORIES SWEPT ASIDE LIKE DRY LEAVES

Looking back I feel a sense of nostalgia for a world that is no longer here. I look back for old illusions and find they are gone. It is as if the cobwebs of my mind have been swept aside beneath the dust of time. I see that there are many tears and other uncomfortable feelings that I have suppressed for years. Living so long in the shadow of my fears, I now look back and wonder.

If only there was a map to self-understanding. But there are no signposts to the future. There are no guarantees we have learned the karmic lessons from our past, no matter how brutal these lessons have been. For some reason, humans are like tires with treads marked by patterns of living as they roll over and over and over repeating the inculcated patterns that are there.

When I search my past, I remember the summer days of my teen years when I walked barefoot on the grass. Sometimes, in the sun, I read a book under a tree. I would look at the sea and sky and dream my dreams. It was a time when I floated on the summer lakes and the summer sunlight filled my days with hope and joy.

These days, I often try to search for what was buried so deeply inside myself that it turned my life and marriage into a horror story. When I was a teen, I loved the world. My senses were alive to the beauty all around, the sights, the smells, the wind, the sun and the rain. I never had an inkling that my future husband would chase me through dark, snow-filled nights trying to beat my brains out or punch the daylights out of me while I ran screaming and alone into the night looking for the police. I never believed that I would cower in my room when I heard him screaming and ready to strike me or one of my children. When I think of this, a sadness settles over me and hovers like a rain cloud ready to break. There are tears behind my eyes and if I try to recapture dreams of hope they all seem to have vanished forever.

I often wish I had my teen dreams again. I wish I could believe the beautiful fantasies I once built, but, unfortunately, I cannot. I do not even take pride in the suffering I have endured. At this moment in time, as I listen to music and stare at the globe light on my bookcase and at the hundreds of books I once hungrily read searching for answers to my life, I wonder what the future holds as I have almost escaped this nightmare that I once lived. Past memories have been swept aside like dry leaves that fall from autumn trees. They are no longer alive with color and I wonder, what now?

I know the past is over. The life I once led and my attachments are gone.

One slim thread of hope unites me with my two sons who are growing up and will soon be men. My friend Ben has been an anchor in this stormy sea, and a lifeline, a continuum. At moments when I believed I could not endure, he stood by with love and faith in the power of life's miracles and with an endless compassion for the bottomless pain that seemed never-ending in my soul.

For it is a friend that we truly need. He heard my cries and tried to help me forget my tears. He had the vision to show me the joy within myself and to allow me to live with my sadness. I wish the world were filled with people who could let others be who they really are and still care for them. Sometimes, my soul raged. I believed I was going mad with pain. I watched in disbelief at the hurt that had been inflicted upon me and I would go to Ben's house on the water and look out at Connecticut. There all the tears and pain could hang out in a safe space. Getting a divorce after being battered in my marriage I had to relearn living again because I felt so much pain and humiliation. I needed to trust and to feel safe again. Ben's house provided a sanctuary in this frightening whirlwind and collision of all my dreams and dashed hopes.

I just felt frozen and backed into the strangest kind of aloneness. I felt so alone, like nothing I had ever known. I wanted to get past feeling alone, alienated and unable to trust, but I could not. I could not share the strangeness of my life with most people. Usually they blame the victim which shows how little they understand of this wife-abuse phenomenon. I wanted to share love again, but there was too much grief and too much fear for that to happen.

Every time I felt better, it turned up like a ghost floating near me. The words: "You can't be happy, you can't be free," echoed in my ears as sadness bombarded my body. I was now like a wounded bird lying in a clump on the ground. It was as if I had fallen from a very high branch and because I couldn't fly, I now needed to learn to fly again. My knowledge of flight had been crushed on my descent as I lay in a heap on the ground. I didn't want to feel like a wounded bird. I wanted to climb and fly and sing and float through the air lightly and gracefully. But I bore witness to myself on the ground with a broken set of wings, lying in the dirt.

I tried to make the world over again to fit my dreams. It didn't work. What counted was the reality I had to face. I needed to heal from experiences in the past. We can carry dreams around forever, but chasing rainbows, building castles in the air, dreaming dreams and believing all our fantasies and stories did not help. For this, I ended with a set of broken wings because I needed to learn to fly again.

Now I ask why I did not write this book long ago? This story should have been written ages ago. Why did I wait so long to give voice to my silence? Why did I endure so much pain and madness and not articulate this criminal behavior so others could learn from my mistakes? Why did I stop myself from living a life that was truly of my own choice?

Chapter 49

THE SINGLES SCENE

Added to the daily strain of being a liberated lady executive who rides the LIRR at 7:09 and being an ex-wife and current Ivy League mother, I am also new at the singles scene. Having just been pronounced legally separated the 'singles' scene after twenty years of marriage looks like a leper colony to me. First there are the women who tell me there are no men around. As they whine through their relentless tale of deserted, man-less Madhattan, I am suffering incredible guilt.

Whatever it is, I can't find a place to be left alone. There seem to be men all over the place, and they're always trying to pick me up on trains. I wear this Garbo look, hoping that I can get from my office to my home without any pickups. I even wear my wedding band to insure safe passage through the entrails of the bar car of the LIRR. But that doesn't stop the hordes. If I looked like Gina Lollobrigida or Marilyn I'd understand, but I'm perimenopausal, as my doctor calls it, and not particularly special.

That's what baffles me! Either that or I look like everybody's mother or lost Aunt Sadie. It's OK when a man my own age or older picks me up, but when they're all ten years younger or more, then I don't know what to do.

The singles scene is filled with doom and gloom—forty-seven women for every male. Every time I've gone to one of those place I've ended up like Auntie Mame—matchmaking. For some unknown reason, everyone loves their misery. They all protest that they want and need a relationship but complain how hard it is to get one started. Well, it is, if you hide in your apartment. But then again, people are afraid.

Fear permeates the singles scene. Everyone is acting so cool because underneath they are scared to death that they will make the same mistake again. Why shouldn't they be scared? You only have one life to give to the great rip off institution called marriage and once burned, you'll be a little more cautious the second time. After all, your total identity is at stake, your Pepsodent smile, Clairol hair, Givenchy scarf, not to speak of your inner self-concept.

In a society where the 'be all and end all' of living is not to be ALONE, marriage is the pinnacle of accomplishment for women—and divorce the scourge of my generation. So—what has a single person left to feel good about? They got the message! They are losers! After all, any woman worth anything is married! People who are alone aren't worth much. They are devalued merchandise. Somehow I bought into that value system. It got to me before I was three. Did you ever watch three-year-olds in nursery school? Everyone is getting married. Little girls are serving coffee to the three-year-old boys in the play kitchen. Who told them to do this? After all, they're only three years old!

Somewhere, we've gotten the message. So, the singles scene is for losers because, in this best of all possible worlds, only married people count. Let's sweep everyone else under the rug. Of course that means that most newly divorced and separated single men and women are compensating for a horrible sense of inadequacy. It's as if they have to apologize to everyone because their marriage busted up. Mostly, they have to get their own heads together, and that isn't easy because they are already their own best enemy. Everyone else just adds fuel to the fire, and the wonder is that these people don't end up basket cases for all the support, love and acceptance they never get from others. Many of them never recover from this trauma. Some of them never forgive themselves or their spouses.

When you tell a guy you're separated, his eyes light up like neon signs: after all, you must want to fool around. That's why I still wear my wedding band. It's the best protection a single woman can carry when she ventures forth into the singles scene. It gives you a little leverage. You can decide who you want to go out with, and only let the eligible males you wish to know know that you are single.

Chapter 50

WHY DO SENIORS LOOK 28? WHAT IS HAPPENING TO OLD PEOPLE?

When people ask me how I am it's hard to answer because right now I don't even know WHO I am. I used to know who I was a few years ago. I was wife, mother, lover—but now the whole thing is up for grabs. There are days when I feel like Dorothy in the *Wizard of Oz*, and other days when I feel like Grandma Moses. You could say that I've lost my equilibrium.

I am no longer acculturated. My role is not predestined. I can be anything and everything because I am FREE! But what a scary word free is. Strange, the men I know in their fabulous forties and fifties are going through even stranger experiences than I am. They have become flower children—chasing after twenty-year-olds, losing their identities and generally suffering from the greatest blight of our society: the desire to escape getting older. The two greatest blights we face today are divorce and the fear of aging.

It's OK to get divorced if you stay twenty-five for the rest of your life. But God forbid you should age, grow a gray hair or lose your size eight dress line—watch out! Danger ahead. Almost like *Jaws*, beaches where sharks abound—there is great danger! There are no senior citizens in this amazing country of ours—or at least there are none who look it. Not in Mad Hasset, Great Neck, Washed Port. Maybe some can be found in the coal mining towns of Pennsylvania or the upper reaches of British Columbia, but not in Mad Manhattan. The glamour center of the world supports only youthful, stylish 'femmes' and 'hommes' who never age and who can keep their tennis tans year round. They seem to look younger with each passing year. Have you ever wondered what is happening to old people? They seem to be getting younger all the time. But that is only half the story; the other half is that young people are getting older—much earlier. Why has the world turned upside down? I don't know, but take a closer look at the next forty- or fifty-year-old you meet. Why do they all look twenty-eight? And why does the great unwashed generation of teenagers look like they're going on forty?

This brings me to my next theory. If everyone gets younger as they get older then maybe the time for romance should begin when people reach mid-life crisis. Maybe everyone has to start over again, having learned from their childish mistakes. Perhaps our next generation will marry for a period of time, but not forever because with an increasing life span, people would die early if they had to live for their entire, long lives with one spouse that caused them unhappiness. Maybe it's time to break the chain that holds a lot of people captive in misery based upon marriage mythology. Behind many smiling masks may be lurking two murderously vengeful humans who would kill each other if they would not get caught. But they keep on smiling!

So when people ask me how I am, I haven't got a ready answer. I can say I'm looking for myself. I got lost on the way to my wedding at the Fifth Avenue Hotel twenty years ago. I've put in twenty years of time just like an inmate in a penitentiary and what have I got to show for it? Two Ivy League sons, five cats, one large white elephant house and one slightly aging perimenopausal body with worry lines around my forehead. (This was written before botox!)

Why worry lines? Because I don't know where I fit and I am still searching for love and peace and a sense of safety on this planet which will probably choke in its own pollution before too long.

Each day spreads its newness near me and seems like a jigsaw puzzle that I cannot always put together. I feel like I'm laughing from a distant star and wondering how and when all the pieces of the puzzle will fit together. Or, if they ever will. I keep trying to figure out what all the divine discontent is about and how humanity will plug the dike before we all drown in illusion and confusion.

Chapter 51

MY SONS, THE ROCK STARS

All memories are buried with the dissolution of my marriage. My sons and I spread apart to live in different places linked by a bond of love and I always feel the tears come as I look down on the ground. I never could find a four leaf clover; in all the years I searched, I never found even one. One day walking in the park I was still hoping to find one lucky clover. But I had not found one. So I walked back to my apartment.

Last year I moved out of the house, but my children still returned to it in the summer after their college classes were over. Their father had to pay the mortgage—one step towards involving him in more responsibility. It had been painful for me to leave, but with both children off to college most of the year, I knew I couldn't get my life together without trying to live alone. So I rented an apartment.

My apartment was to be a place where I put myself back together again. It worked for a while, but then I lapsed. Independence was O.K., but all the anguish of the past came with me and at times I felt the walls closing in on me. I had been searching, searching, searching and finding nothing. I just crawled into my own little corner and felt like a wounded animal licking my wounds.

I had had my share of violence, Greek tragedy, Russian sociodrama and now, at last, I was going to find happiness in the wide, wide world, all alone. But I am not the type of person who feels best alone. For me, trying to be independent and happy were long orders for a person, like myself, who was short on both independence and happiness.

While I was searching for myself, my oldest son decided that Ivy League colleges were for non-creative people. He was now going to discover himself in a new persona—as a musician. If you want to see middle-class parents on the brink—just let them find out their eldest son, the potential lawyer or doctor, has just decided to become a famous rock star.

After my musical friends had all given me their condolences, I pulled myself together to talk to my son who by now had used up some of his hard—earned money to outfit himself with a slick electric guitar, embroidered strap and expensive amps.

We talked.

"Why didn't you tell me you wanted music lessons when you were little? I would have given them to you."

"Listen, mom, if you'd given me music lessons when I was little, I probably wouldn't want to be a musician today."

"But you've never had a music lesson in your life—you're going to have to start from scratch."

"That's O.K. It's not where I am now, it's where I'm gonna be. I KNOW where I'm gonna be. So don't worry."

Me, not worry? I had visions of him riding the rails, guitar in hand, playing sleazy little clubs, starving to death—regretting having given up his career as a potential Ivy League judge or some such august profession.

He interrupted my thoughts. "I'm willing to make sacrifices, mom, for my music. Believe me, I'm willing to give it all I have . . . to . . . to be a musician."

I was quietly shaken.

"Oh, it's great to be creative."

"Why does everyone sound so cheerful when I say I want to be a musician? When I told grandpa long distance he didn't sound overjoyed. Well, I'm going to devote every minute of my life to my music," he said. And he did just that. I think he took his finals in a maze of bar chords and the sounds of the Beatles, broken guitar strings and his new compositions ringing inside his head rather than with any interest in his class work at Columbia College. Fortunately, he got his usual excellent grades, and I breathed a sigh of relief.

By this time he had moved home from the dorms with his guitar, amps, stereo and records. The neighbors, I must say, were tolerant of the local noise as the new, fledgling musician on the block practiced ten to twelve hours a day. The cats seemed charmed by the music and their reaction may be understandable because they wouldn't know an 'off' note from an 'on' note.

During these months, I think my son spent all his food money on guitar lessons. He was determined to 'make it.' In the usual fashion of a middle-class mother on the brink of a divorce and nervous breakdown at the same time, I wanted to see my children's lives secure and happy since mine had not been. So the image of a musician's life set up such a feeling of insecurity that I finally decided to grin and bear it for the next ten years or more, or until he did make it, or hopefully found another medium of artistic expression.

As he explained, he couldn't see himself riding the LIRR in grey flannel, and he really, really loved music. Life is full of unexpected twists, and this certainly was. As I entered my apartment after a nostalgic visit to the park, I was greeted by the phone ringing. It was my son who asked if I wanted to come over for his concert.

It had been four months since he had started his musical career. I went over to the house which was always painful because of all the nasty memories that clung like ghosts to every inch of the walls. I sat out on the back lawn and he and his younger brother began to play. The music was beautiful and as I smiled through my tears, I blinked in the sunlight disbelieving life's strange patterns, the force of human will and strength.

They were terrific, enthusiastic musicians. It was a joy to hear them. Their happiness radiated as they played and sang. The neighborhood resounded to the music coming off the amps, the cats sat like sentinels on the lawn, wiser and more knowing than I. And I relaxed and listened to the beauty of their youth and joy. My sons were dancing and singing with joy at what they felt. I realized that life's unexpected twists were always lights into the unknown. I had finally found a four leaf clover, and it was right there in my own backyard.

Chapter 52

BORN CHASSIDIC, CONVERTED TO

CHRISTIAN SCIENCE

Looking around my house is enough to make me dive back into bed under the quilts. It looks like a blitzkrieg. Having never been a model housekeeper, years of children, chaos and cats have not added any order to my home.

My bedroom is still a relic of aging bookshops, paperback clutter and term papers from my graduate degree (taken frenziedly three years ago in order to be licensed to teach and feed my children, the cats and myself). Having begun my marriage with the intention of being a mother-writer or writing-mother, I had to juggle the children, cooking and reading all at the same time. So my bedroom began to look like the London Blitz about ten years ago. The only people allowed into the sanctum sanctorum of my bedroom are very close relatives, and the cats (because they can't tell anybody what sort of housekeeper I am). My very close relatives include me—and sometimes, my sons.

My mother would be carried out on a stretcher if she saw the upstairs of my house. So, fortunately, she lives in San Francisco and when she visits she doesn't like to climb stairs. She may, however, have an inkling about the bedroom because when she visits the kitchen she starts washing dishes and pots and pans. If I ask her what she's doing, she just says, "You need help!"

I sure do.

About three years ago the dishwasher disposal got clogged and when the repairman came he tried to fix it. However after he fixed it the machine wouldn't release water. I finally decided to leave well enough alone and do the dishes by hand, and then have it fixed when I could find ninety free dollars. Until one day my ex-husband in a fit of kindness decided to pay for a repairman to fix the dishwasher. I think that was because when he came to the house he couldn't find any clean dishes. I only wash dishes once a week and that's on Saturday nights.

After suggesting paper plates he called the repair service. The next week I received a frantic phone call from him at my office explaining that he had planned a surprise for my birthday. Knowing his usual propensity for lousing things up I screamed, "What?"

"I was going to fix the dishwasher as a birthday present for you—BUT . . ."

"But what?" I choked, knowing it had to be his usual mess-up.

"The repairman banged something and the motor is still turned on, but it's totally wiped out. We have to cut the wires or there'll be electricity drawn into the washer—and it's full of water."

"And I can get electrocuted."

"I had him cut the wires—so, you won't get electrocuted."

By now I looked like a stroke victim. Choking, I said, "Thanks for the present!"

"You're welcome."

"Now the dishwasher can never be repaired, right?"

"Uh huh."

"So now I have to buy a new one?"

"Uh huh!"

"And I can't afford a new one!"

"Right."

"Thanks for the happy birthday."

I slammed down the phone. So that's why I have no dishwasher. When I get rich, I will buy one.

I live in absolute terror that the refrigerator will die on me. I can wash dishes, but no way can I cool food by hand. As for the freezer, there's always the danger that it too will go, and my investment in Wednesday bargains at the supermarket may go with it.

When my furnace went, I was sure that I would not live to see another winter in Great Neck. The estimates for fixing the furnace ran from $1,000 down to $10. We finally settled on $250 when the smaller estimates were not really going to fix anything, but were just "to look." When the time came to pay up, my husband borrowed his half from me and said he would pay it back. We all went on austerity for a couple of weeks, but the house was warm.

My life in Great Neck was a succession of successful negotiations.

The oil company usually sends the truck to fill the furnace only if I guarantee the man will be handed a check for the next bill. If I can't, they tell me my pipes are going to blow up. They call me whenever they fear for my house—since, when the gauge gets down to empty, they know it's time to explain our credit situation once again.

The telephone company is a little better. They give me ten days' grace after the phone bill is due. In the years of my marriage my husband managed to elude so many creditors that the credit scene becomes dismal if his name is even mentioned in the vicinity of fifty miles. Since I still have his name and the same address I usually receive the snake charmers reaction to the sound of his credit rating.

"No credit!"

Having hassled through several winters of agony trying to balance miniscule amounts of money in my checkbook and keeping track of which checks have been cashed and which have not, I've become an unwelcome sight at the bank.

"Mrs. G, we simply can't provide personalized service for you. If we did this for all our customers, the bank would go bankrupt."

"But you don't."

"We can't."

The bank officer is usually ready to throw a potted geranium at me when he sees me. He feels once I've written a check, I should consider the money spent. What he doesn't understand is that several days' grace on an un-cashed check might feed my cats and kids.

The young students at the bank are my friends, and they always help me out. Probably because my bank balance and theirs look very much alike. Who else but a student in the affluent suburb of Great Neck would be caught dead with a bank balance like mine? Certainly not the mini-skirted ladies on the tennis courts.

While I freeze in winter, they are wrapped in mink. While I battle to find enough money to feed my kids and cats, they're sunning themselves in Acapulco or the West Indies.

Since my kids go to school with their kids—there must be some kind of divine justice! Or is God just up there laughing at me because I had the misfortune to be born a Chassid, and am ready to become a Christian Scientist? (No other religion can claim to have been founded by a woman.)

It's not that I am really an ardent woman's libber, but it's nice to feel some kind of liberation from the damn daily problems I face. It seems to me liberation might take the form of a protective husband who could save me from the 7:09 on the LIRR, or the ulcer attacks in my office when the place is about to self destruct.

Chapter 53

CHEERS FOR THE LIRR

Just when I am ready to go to California for my nervous breakdown my brother has invited me to stay at his home in San Francisco. Why not? My brother is the West Coast aficionado in the broken marriage and nervous breakdown syndrome that I am on the East Coast.

Let me explain. My brother and his Danish girlfriend never married, saving themselves untold grief and hardship. Since they have managed to live together in love, peace and harmony for ten years, they've got it all over most of the marriages I know.

The invitation to have my nervous breakdown on the West Coast is a tempting one, and I will as soon as I find the time. Right now, I have so many bills to pay, including fuel oil, I can't afford one. (But it remains an option in the back of my mind as one way out). You see, on the West Coast, everybody is divorced or shacking up and a divorced mother of two teenage sons would easily fit into that way of life.

Not so on the East Coast. Here you are mistaken for DRACULA! Since the support system for newly-un-weds is lacking, one relies on friends, relatives and the LIRR for access to male attention. This is fine if you have a lot of friends and relatives, and ride back and forth on the railroad at least five times a day (costly as it may seem it could be considered an investment in one's future).

There's more than one millionaire on the LIRR. Reactions to riding the railroad vary from, "Ugh," and "I hate it," to non-committal shrugs.

I, for one, want to stand up and cheer for the LIRR! As any woman well knows the ratio of males to females on that railroad is about 10,000 to 1. What other situation can offer such odds to a woman? Added to that is the fact that most of the men who ride are fairly successful, i.e. there's more than one millionaire to be had for the price of a commuter ticket.

I do, however, have my own ground rules. Others may do as they please. Married men are off limits! Having lived through the pangs of separation and, hopefully, of divorce I wouldn't in any way, shape or form engage in the male chauvinist pig transaction known as the "affair" or the "mistress syndrome" which is filled with so many rotten connotations for any honest woman's libber. Why should I hurt one of my sisters? Besides, if I had to suffer the pangs of legal separation and the breakup of my marriage, why should Mr. "No guts" be spared if he already hates his wife and she, of course, doesn't understand him.

So, mixed into this spectacular breed of corrupt, inconsequential male ego and power are a few genuine human beings. The divorced male on the Gold Coast of Long Island Sound is a breed unto himself. He has been shattered and thrust into stardom without any warning and is in total shock. He is therefore filled with anger at the opposite sex. But does he know it? No!

He therefore comes on helpless, but watch out because behind that exterior is a sex-starved lusting male who will stop at nothing to get a woman into his bed. Now, that may be fine for some women, but the truth is that he makes a very unsound marriage prospect because he is also in a state of total confusion.

The only thing to do is stay cool and keep laughing because life is full of strange quirks. Added to the sex-starved divorced and married males on the LIRR, there also exist the sex-starved single ladies. The lady is wearing blinders because she will march around groaning that there aren't any men in this world. I suppose you could say that about suburbia, but you can't say that about the LIRR. That's why I say, "Cheers for the Long Island Railroad!"

Chapter 54

INTERNATIONAL WOMAN'S YEAR

My lady boss at the social agency that I worked for decided to holiday in Hong Kong. Sounded like a great idea until we found out that the next year's annual budget was due in a few days and she hadn't put it together. A few of us courageous souls said, "Not to worry, we'll do the budget for her." I stayed at Martha's apartment for several nights because we were working well into the night at the office trying to put in all the budget details for the next year.

There were a lot of questions that we couldn't answer but we winged it all the way. We had to put in everyone's salaries and benefits for the next year and we just kept right on putting in every number we knew we could get into the budget. By the third day, without much sleep, we had finished something. We called her in Hong Kong to find out when she was returning. She said, "In two weeks." Well, everything would be done by then and she'd have to find ways to live with our budget.

Martha and I were to attend International Woman's Year at the United Nations. Women from all over the world were in attendance including a nursing mother who was asked to leave because she was nursing in an open forum. She refused to leave and was escorted out by security. I wanted so much to see all the dignitaries like Betty Friedan and Germaine Greer from Australia as well as the Russian lady cosmonaut who brought out a group of nesting dolls and other crafts for all to see. There were many speeches by notable women from around the world and yet, though I had been looking forward to this day for a long time, I had all I could do to keep my eyes open. Betty Friedan was two rows in front of me and as she spoke, I found myself falling asleep. I couldn't keep my eyes open because I was so tired from having stayed up every night to finish that budget with Martha. Now all I could do was attempt to stay awake—an impossible task.

I had looked forward to this amazing day, which was unfortunately spoiled by the exhaustion I felt. I tried as much as I could not to fall asleep in an obvious way, but I really don't remember too much that happened that day. For the first time the world was celebrating women and encouraging their accomplishments. It was a moment to be remembered and I do believe I slept through most of it.

The International Women's Year celebration at the UN was the culmination of years of change. The culmination of work by women around the world who said they wanted peace and a better world for their children and for all women everywhere.

As I sat there dozing I remembered back to when I was pregnant with my older son and we were all 'gung ho' to change New York City. This particular night we were invited to a Democratic Party local meeting held in the headquarters basement. Mrs. Eleanor Roosevelt and former Governor Herbert Lehman were coming to talk to us about getting corruption out of Tammany Hall and restoring responsible government to New York by putting in a clean sweep of new people to run the city.

In my life, I have been extremely fortunate to meet Hubert Humphrey and then Governor Bill Clinton. At this time, it was indeed a privilege to meet Eleanor Roosevelt, who came to talk with us and asked us to fight to clean up the corruption in New York City and oust the people who'd taken the government away from the people.

All my friends were going to try to run for political office. We started programs on the upper East and West sides of Manhattan, and the local club leaders were holding meetings to educate the populace in the local neighborhoods.

One of the people in the group was Theodore Weiss who had never run for any political office before. He was born in Hungary and had come to the US as an immigrant to escape the Holocaust. He needed to obtain enough signatures to be put on the ballot and to run for political office. Having just finished Law School he was planning to go door to door to obtain these signatures but he needed a woman to go with him because women at home were not likely to open their doors to a man who had come alone.

My friend Lolly and I took turns going with him, and since we were both pregnant it was a good time to be helping out with the election.

We called him Teddy and he did get on the ballot and then won a seat on the New York City Council where he served for many years. He eventually became head of the New York City Council and made many fine contributions to better governance for the city.

As Lolly and I began to offer programs for the community in midtown Manhattan, we developed a "self help program" which in time was brought to Washington, DC and ultimately became one of Lyndon Johnson's Great Society programs. It was a volatile time for all of us. John F. Kennedy was assassinated and the country went into shock.

I remembered back to the local Congressional election and the potential candidates who wanted to run came to meet with the leaders of the Democratic Party in our apartment. Selection for the local Congressional election was held in my apartment. A series of candidates presented their approaches to the club representatives who would decide and vote amongst themselves for the next candidate to be put on the ballot for the party. Every forty-five minutes a new potential candidate came to the door, and another one left after their presentation.

That evening Paul O' Dwyer, brother of the former mayor of New York City, was in my kitchen. I think he had come a bit early and needed to wait his turn out of earshot from the living room. At the time he was seeking to run for the Congressional seat. Five potential candidates met one at a time with the Democratic Club representatives. I chatted in the kitchen while potential candidates waited to be interviewed. They rang the bell almost every half hour or forty-five minutes for their interview. Finally they chose Bill Ryan as the Congressional candidate and O' Dwyer did not get selected that particular year.

It was an exciting time. I had my first child and within a few years we tried to follow Eleanor Roosevelt's wishes and advice, but so much suddenly changed. Within a few years we witnessed so many assassinations. I remember my older son crying as he came home from kindergarten devastated at Kennedy's assassination. He sat in front of the TV for days watching the coverage. In a few years the assassination of Martin Luther King and Robert Kennedy followed in a country numbed by these events.

My son remembers when he was a year and a half and saw John Kennedy and Jackie waving to the crowds along Broadway. Little as he was, he waved back. He heard the cheering as the motorcade drove down the middle of Broadway. His father held him high on his shoulders so he could see John Kennedy. I believe I was pregnant with my second son at the time, and the crowds waving and shouting were an inspiration as sound echoed through the streets of New York. It was a time when there was still great hope for the future.

Chapter 55

PATHS TO CONSCIOUSNESS

The world is proliferating paths to consciousness too fast. I can hardly keep up with their names. In the last few days I have heard of several systems I hadn't heard about before. They all sound linked in some mystical way by a set of gestalts. There is such a range of descriptions and so many exotic details, I have to keep learning new definitions just to keep up with all these psycho-therapies, religions and humanistic concepts.

Last week, I heard about Rolfing, Patterning and Biobalancing, in addition to Swedish Earth Massage, Karmic Massage and Indian Massage. The last three always make me cry. I don't know why but massages make me upset and tearful. In addition the therapists who practice these body therapies usually hate talking and are reluctant to shed light on the mysteries they practice. But I figure if I keep asking questions they will eventually reveal why they do what they do. In addition, my friend who is fully convinced that bioenergetics is the total answer keeps asking me to breathe—breathe—BREATHE!

One thing they all have in common is the demand that you BREATHE! And that includes Hatha Yoga, too. All exercises related to body work are involved in the increased awareness of breathing, sensitivity to one's body, and the opening of the tube inside us that we close up from childhood. This tube connects our eating functions to our sexual functioning to our excretory functions.

The premise is that if we are all locked up in these areas of our bodies and the energy will not flow freely, the body will become prey to illnesses, blocks, pain and negativities that would not be there if the body were in balance with all its natural functions.

It is a very simple theory and very important because it seeks to align the physical body with the functions intended. If we do not accept the purpose of the body and its intended work then we sabotage it's natural flow of energies—and voilà, we self destruct.

The only problem with all these beautiful theories is that they are extremely costly! Therefore, if only the rich can be cured, where does that leave the masses of poor people? They are then left with constipation, back troubles, ulcers, migraine headaches and colitis. The question really is : is it only the wealthy who can be given the tools for good health, or is it going to be made available to the poor souls on this earth who can't plunk down thousands for these remedies?

My continuing search goes on and on. After Rolfing there is Acupuncture, Patterning, Bioenergetics, Zen Massage, Reichian therapy and all the massages from many countries such as Thai massage as well as Russian sweat baths. I believe that I must be prepared for any bodily encounter imaginable. I try to laugh at this, but frankly, this always brings me to tears and I don't know why. One thing is for sure, I've never felt certain and secure about my body.

To me, the physical body is always a threat because it is so vulnerable. It is not easily subject to control and we suffer costly pains for our errors.

All the therapies that seek to redirect these energies are, I believe, on the right track. After years of analysis, I have learned only that I still suffer massive feelings of inferiority, a terrible sense of not belonging and the desire to direct my energies outward. Now, in the middle of this large number of recipes for body awareness, there are some benefits and one is, you feel better after all this body work and exercise.

If you are breathing deeply you don't have to feel depressed because in bioenergetics if you feel bad, the first thing you can do is scream, kick, hit and beat out the feelings that are locked up in your body that originated long ago. Other therapies that address this are primal scream therapy and if you need an audience there is always Est and Actualizations.

I find myself exploring so many forms of therapy because there are times when I feel dizzied by these many approaches to the human being. I just wish I could find one answer that worked for me. Right now nothing has been the answer and the more I explore, the more I wonder. Many people have found their own brand of nectar and it seems they should all be experiencing a form of bliss. However, that doesn't seem to be happening. A lot of these people are scraping life at the bottom of the barrel and feeling pretty lousy. They go through the motions of life, but there is a kind of emptiness, a flatness, a sense that all the seeking, searching and dreaming are just other illusions.

Like the victims of the snake-oil peddlers of the past, we can construct any reality we choose to imagine and load it with significance that may not actually exist. Personally, I feel a strange quality as I watch this circus of seeking, searching, exploiting and game playing. I feel I've played the ultimate game for all time, the life and death game, and I have no desire to play any more games. Life is too short!

When you hook into someone else's game, you waste a lot of time. You are deterred from experiencing anything real and it is exhausting because it takes you away from your own center of being. Then you must brush yourself off because it inevitably turns destructive and you have to start all over again, a little the worse for wear and tear on your nervous system.

I'm not advocating avoiding life, but avoiding neurotic games is valuable because if you are involved in neurotic games, you will miss life. And then what? All these superlative rays of consciousness have hit me since I began to break out of the prison of my marriage which was more like a jail than a relationship. I am still trying to sort out what is real and what is unreal.

It seems when a middle-aged person seeks to be single after many years in the cocoon of marriage, their new life choices are up to them. They can choose to become crazy—many people do that. They can do it subtly or self-destruct in sneaky ways—too much liquor, too much sex, too many tranquilizers, too much work, too much running around. After that they are clobbered with a terrible sense of endless emptiness. What they are seeking to run away from is themselves and their own damaged self concepts. Why don't they just own up to their own feelings about themselves? At this moment in time I am ready to admit my sense of failure about myself and my marriage. After all, trying is not enough. Success is the only measure we and society use and by that yardstick I have certainly failed. As a Zen master would say to me: "So what?!"

By what standards are we to measure ourselves in human terms? What value can we place upon our meager, individual lives? Can we live for some greater principle than our own infinitesimal existence? I don't know the answers, and I don't know if I will ever have the answers, but I do have a lot of questions.

Chapter 56

VOLKSWAGEN RABBIT—OR BUST!

Many months have passed since Christmas and New Year's Eve. I've learned to live more on my own. Even the hungry cats seem friendly when I pass them in the house. There are still critical moments, such as when my son decided that I needed to buy him a car last month. Listening to him, I tried to keep a semblance of calm.

Some semblance is about the size of it. College was out of session and the first week back from school my son informed me that the family car was a "death trap." He also stated that he could not get to his three summer jobs without a car. For in his zeal to get enough money for college he had gotten a day job, a night job, and a lunchtime job.

But his father had not put the car in working order, even though he had told him he would need it since January. Naturally, I was called upon the scene as the lifeboat was about to capsize. I had no idea of the symbolic meaning that a car holds for an eighteen-year-old male until I received a frantic phone call at work.

For a beginning, my son said: "You'll never see me again. I can't take any more of dad's games. He told me to get a summer job that I could use public transportation to get to. I'm running away."

My son, whose normal state of equilibrium was rather high, seemed to be losing his marbles. I gulped in the middle of my usual office crises.

"It's only a car we're talking about," I said. "Let's get a car!"

He gasped.

"You're kidding. You can't afford a car."

This was absolutely true, but I wasn't going to let that stop me. I was so angry with his father for doing his usual number on my son that I could have shaken the stuffing out of him if he had been within ten feet of me.

"Let's talk about it when I get home," I gulped.

"If I *am* home," he said. "I have to drive this death trap. I'm taking my life in my hands every time I drive it."

My hands were cold and clammy. I was in shock.

"See you soon. Talk to you tonight," I said and I hung up.

I raced home that night to find my son Keith had driven to work and wouldn't be back until ten p.m. I waited anxiously for him to return.

As he entered the house, I was suddenly barraged with all kinds of auto information he had collected. I was relieved that he had made it home safely after the conversation we had in the afternoon. Keith had thoroughly researched his car problem and suggested we visit the Volkswagen dealer on Saturday.

"Sure," I said, figuring if the cats didn't eat for one year, I could meet some of the car payments.

Jonah and Keith were going to get extra jobs to pay for the car's upkeep. I was presented with several issues of *Consumer Reports,* articles from sports magazines and the information that the Volkswagen Rabbit was the nearest thing to a Mercedes Benz—that is, for a low-priced car. My head was spinning because I know nothing about cars. I don't even drive. On Saturday morning we visited the dealer and he immediately thought I was a well-heeled Nassau County female. I played it cool because I needed credit to purchase this car for my son. So I let him think I was rich!

The next day when I called he said, "Mrs. G, the bank turned you down for credit."

"Why, my credit is fine. I always pay my bills!" I gasped.

"They said slow payment and litigation!"

"That's not me, that's my ex husband."

"Oh, that makes a difference. Why didn't you tell me—they gave me *his* credit rating."

I was now mad as hell. I didn't even have my own identity. My husband's rotten credit rating was still following me.

"I want that wiped out. The reason I'm divorcing him is that he never paid the bills—I don't want to be punished for *his* behavior. I am myself—get a new credit check on *me*, Ms. Ada Garwood."

The salesman heard me. "I can't go back to that bank, but I'll get you credit somewhere else—don't worry. I just can't mention your husband's name to them."

I nodded. He wasn't kidding. I was shaking with rage at being dogged by this mess.

"Call me tomorrow," said the salesman, "I'll have the information for you."

"O.K."

Meanwhile my son called me three times a day at work to see if the credit had been approved.

"Not yet," I said, as he subtly reminded me that every hour he drove that smoking, broken-down car was a risk to his life. The following day I called the car dealer who informed me that I had received credit and could buy the car. He said he hadn't mentioned my husband's name and credit had been granted in a few hours.

"Wow! What a relief."

I was ready to buy the car just to prove I was a good credit risk. It's not easy for single women to get credit—even if they are over forty and have a son in college. My anger about female identity when not married had hit an all time high. I realized that during the years of my marriage I hadn't existed and any credit rating I received was a reflection of my husband's behavior. I was spitting mad! Every young woman must establish her own <u>identity</u> right away and keep it. If she decides to marry and be considered no more than a longhorn steer by society then she risks not being bankable. This was thirty years ago and I think things have changed since that time—or at least, I hope they have.

My son was overjoyed because he was getting a car, and I—I was white as a ghost trying to figure out how to meet the payments. My paycheck wasn't stretching very far these days, and with college tuition, broken appliances and cat food, I was near a nervous breakdown. I felt like a lamb being led to slaughter.

The next night I called a friend who said, "You sound funny."

"Who me, why should I sound funny? I just bought a car, that's all."

"You just bought a car? I'm coming over to take you to my house—you sound funny."

When she arrived, I was in pretty bad shape. The truth was I hadn't slept since this car tragedy began and that was about six nights back.

At her house she poured me a glass of wine. "Relax," she said.

"Sure, I'm relaxed."

"You can't afford a car."

"I know," and I spilled out the whole gruesome story. She didn't say anything until the end, when she said, "I have a better idea."

"What?"

"I'll tell you later."

When her husband came home she pulled him into the other room, and when they both came back together she said, "You're not buying a car."

I was punchy by this time.

"I'm not?"

"No, we're giving you a car."

I sat there in shock.

"You see, we have four cars in the driveway, and there's no room. You can have our daughter's old car."

"I can?"

I couldn't answer. I was ready to cry.

It seemed like a miracle. My life has been made up of tiny miracles that happen when I least expect them to appear. Now the real miracle had to be accomplished. And that was to convince an eighteen-year-old male in the throes of a car romance that an old car was as good as a new Volkswagen Rabbit.

By this time I was exhausted from being mother and father to my teenage sons and was ready for a rest home. There are days when I wish life wasn't filled with so many complications, and there are even times when I'd like to rest. But how?

Someone's got to be willing to pull the oars, or the ship is going to sink, and this ship had five cats, two sons and a white elephant house, plus two cars, one working and one about to collapse, one broken dishwasher and a refrigerator about to die at any moment. All of these attached to my LIRR commuter ticket, the railroad upon which I am going to meet my next husband who had better be a millionaire, or at least an appliance repairman.

Chapter 57

HE WANTS TO DESTROY US! WHEN WILL

THIS NIGHTMARE END?

My older son called last night. "I got dad's message and he is not going to let me succeed. He is going to try to destroy me. It doesn't matter how long I avoid facing this issue or putting it off. He will not let us rest."

My body tightened as I heard Keith's message. I had had an earlier phone call from my ex-husband. He said, "Someone stole my briefcase with the keys to the house in it. The children can bring their belongings to your house until I change the locks."

But that was only the tip of the iceberg. I knew that he couldn't let my older son finish Columbia College without disrupting his life and without threatening to destroy him. I was shaken because Keith had only six months to graduation. My peace of mind was constantly shattered by the unresolved horror of all the abuse and destruction he continued to try to heap on me.

My son was weeping on the phone. "I'm not sure I can pay much rent or upkeep, I haven't established myself yet."

The fear and sadness was there. All the muscles of my body tightened and I felt like I had the flu. I experienced a sense of exhaustion and withdrawal as I had experienced for so many years when trying to live with my ex in the past. The breakthrough I had been searching for seemed never to arrive. I kept feeling there would be a breakthrough soon. I'd gone into debt so that I could keep on going and help my sons through school. Terror came up inside me. For so long, I had wanted to sell the house. But the children didn't want to, so I left it there. We could sell it later. When was later? Was later now?

My son was weeping. "I got his message, mom, it is very clear. He wants to destroy us. That's what he wants."

I tightened up with pain and thought, "What could we do now?" I needed to think and I couldn't think clearly. All my dreams and ambitions of the past were held in those tight muscles. I knew I had to make enough money to protect my children a bit longer. They were almost ready to spring into independence, but not quite yet. They needed a little more time. All the dependency/ independence equations whirled around inside my head.

My son kept weeping. "He can't let us live. He has to disrupt everything, all the time. I know I have to get away from this man."

I had left. But, now what? Sell the house? Buy another house? Live in the new house? If we sell the house, it will take some time to get the money.

"I have to sue this bastard," my son said. "I can't let him get away with this. He has to meet his responsibilities for my life. That is really the issue."

Somehow or other we could meet the bills all working together under one roof but the past pain came up for me now: the fear, the memories—and yet we could not afford to live separately right now. I really had to make a lot of money to buy my children a house which would help them until they finished school and started out in life. The pain and anger filled me. I felt like running away. What could I do?

They were frightened at being homeless and certain they would have to go to court to impound every cent he collected from his share of the house. Now, this meant more lawyers, more battles. A rotten game, this game of divorce. I just wanted to break free of all this entanglement. I just wanted not to have to face the constant pain and tension.

"We got his message, mom, this house is not safe with him in it. I am not safe in his presence. I've been putting off the decision. I know I have to leave.

But he has responsibilities to meet towards me, his son. Why should I let him get away with it? That's exactly what he wants. Why should I? Why should I?

The bastard."

It was nearly 1:00 a.m. and we had been on the phone for three hours trying to solve this problem. Yet it persisted. I kept feeling a tightening in my arms the longer we talked.

"It's getting late. Maybe we can find a solution tomorrow?"

My son's knee had been hurting. "Maybe I should bring all my belongings over to your place tonight."

"O.K., if you want to."

"At least things will be safe with you."

Damn it—why did this man viciously threaten our entire sense of safety? We knew that eventually we could overcome this. But I was so weary and I didn't feel able to come up with an answer tonight.

My son knew his father would not give us any money towards survival.

There was no love nor loyalty in this man towards his family. He expressed only resentment and refusal. We were like beggars in his eyes.

I wished he would get his head pounded in on some sidewalk in New York City and be done torturing us. My anger goes nowhere if I can't turn it into money to help myself and my children. I just felt so weary and I wanted to curl up and sleep because I was exhausted from the continuous harassment we experienced. When will this nightmare end? When?

Chapter 58

A PACT WITH THE DEVIL

There are no simple solutions to earthly problems. Knots in human systems don't get untied as easily as fishermen's knots. The rules are more complicated. Freedom is always not now. Freedom is always not here. We wait, we struggle. We chase down small dusty paths that seem in the end to be off-purpose from what we intended. Then, we stop, aghast at what lies ahead, afraid to look at the past, trying to find a stopping point, a place to rest, but always time is moving and we cannot rest.

I watch birds fly above the icy sea waters. Peaks of white flash in the windy sea. Out there is a space in the frozen water and my soul floats out looking for a blue sky and wanting to melt into the sun. A melted soul in the plastic age of make believe. We are all part of the great cosmic game of make believe.

The world is heaped with tons of bullshit and we call this life. Tomorrow there will be more pain, more emptiness, more aloneness and more nothingness stretching endlessly out to sea in a world so filled with coldness and lovelessness that this bullshit will freeze us into oblivion.

It seems that we have made a pact with the devil to leave this earth unfulfilled. We have made an agreement not to love—not to be—not to have the best part of life—our humanity.

Chapter 59

JONAH'S HIGH SCHOOL GRADUATION—
"WE SHALL OVERCOME"

Today is an important day. My last child is on his way to college. He will leave the big, old family house and reach out to the world. The house stands like a sentinel in the darkness. I have moved away to an apartment. My sons are still living in the house because they do not want to leave the house they've grown up in. They want to stay.

I understand their feelings. Since it is the only world they've known for most of their lives, the separation from the house is also a separation from childhood, the past they are familiar with and filled with memories they want to hold onto for a while longer. I certainly know how hard it is to give up these memories of childhood. My own memories of childhood still cling to me even at my age.

I wanted them to come with me, but they weren't ready. My oldest son has lived at college for the last two years and now his younger brother is preparing to exit into life. Inside my gut, I feel great loneliness. I want my children with me. It feels like a part of myself is being lost. But they have chosen to stay there for a while. They, too, are preparing to leave in their own way. I feel their agony at this break. What is coming? Where do they belong? The past is coming to a close and my heart aches for them.

I feel all the pain of having had them for too short a time. They have grown into manhood so very fast. Too fast for me. Yet I cannot bring back the early years of their childhood, the smells of their infant years when I held them close to me and loved them generously. Then there was hope and joy, now replaced by aloneness and emptiness. I prepare for my younger son's high school graduation. I fill my purse with tissues and my sunglasses, so the world outside will not see me cry. I am in a fog.

I call my friend Ben. I forget to bring a camera. I'm sure I'll miss the bus, so I leave three hours early. What to wear? Everything seems wrong. I ache with loneliness and pain. Everything is ending. I call Ben because everything feels like it is too much to bear.

"Hello, Ben, I've lost touch with you. Are you there?"

"I'm here."

"I've got to see you. I don't think I'm going to make it through my son's graduation."

He agrees to meet me at the university where the graduation will take place. A pain subsides and a piece of my inner self moves back into place. I have a friend, a real friend. A person who hears my unscreamed screams, who has visions of my future as a bright, golden light and who holds out a source of hope for what is to come.

I try to pull myself together to face the memories, the other parents and the day I cannot face. I board the bus and stare out at the houses as we pass them by, and soon I am there. I arrive at the campus an hour early. I walk upon the green lawns that stretch across Adelphi University where the graduation will take place. I look up at the pale, blue sky and suddenly feel a sense of peace for a moment. If only I could rest a while, if only I could stop running and running and running from my fears.

The graduation begins. The graduating high school seniors are dressed in their caps and gowns. I hear the band play and tears are running down my cheeks. I put on my sunglasses to hide my sorrow. And then the hours go by. My son's name is called and he walks up, handsome and sure, shakes the hand of the principal and turns to the audience and raises his fingers in the sign of victory and peace.

The crowd applauds and through my tears I see that he has given me his message.

"We shall overcome."

He disappears into a crowd of young people to return home with his friends. My ex-husband, as usual, has not paid the car insurance and is looking for a ride home.

I slip away on the green meadows of the campus and look for my friend Ben. I need a friend to pull me past this day. And he is there waiting near his office at the university. The sun is going down. I see him quietly waiting for me and a sense of peace settles over me. Suddenly, I am at home again. Ben knows that I have fled the past, the violence, the sorrow and the terror to try to rebuild my life. He knows all my history and still believes that I can leave it behind and move on.

We walk along the small, grassy, green hills and I hope and pray that the strength I feel with Ben will stay with me when I am alone.

"It's easy," says Ben. "You can leave all the past behind, just let go of it. Don't hang onto it. Let it go."

"I always fear that I will carry the past into the future and fool myself again."

He answers me, but I don't really hear what he says. I can't listen. I'm not ready to be free. I know I have a way to go.

"Where has all the joy in me gone?"

"You are afraid to feel joy—you've been programmed to suffer."

"That's true, I've got to stop the suffering tapes in my head, the victim tapes, the hurt and fear and martyrdom. But I can't."

"When you decide to, you will. Are you ready to give them up right now? Here and now—are you ready to love life now? To live life now?"

"If only I could believe and trust again."

Ben hears me and a wave of strength washes over me like a golden light. I turn to him.

"Ben, you are a—messenger—you carry God's messages."

He listens quietly and says that he knew I would call him this morning.

"How did you know?"

"I kept running across slips of paper with your telephone number yesterday, and I knew I would be hearing from you."

"Ben, you always know when I am in trouble. I wondered why you didn't call."

He doesn't answer me.

"It was good to hear from you," he finally says. "You helped me, too, as I talked with you about your grief—something also healed inside me, as well."

"Thank you for telling me this," I said.

I wonder how my angst could help to heal another soul. But I am happy that the world works like that. Perhaps, I think, if we share ourselves, in truth we can heal the ills of this earth, and the world will achieve a new and higher form of consciousness.

Ben hands me a new story he has written. I glance at the title, "The Centering, A Story of Our Time for the Child of All Ages," and it is about love which he defines as life opening up vibrant energy and life which he says is liberation, integration, fulfillment and enlightenment.

I look at his face. It is the face of a magician in the act of transforming my vision of this world. I accept hope from him as he hands me the gift of his story.

Chapter 60

THE END OF A LONG JOURNEY

Unwittingly Joseph had given me a splendid gift. He shared the morning after the training with my two sons and myself. They came bubbling out of the hotel ballroom at 3 a.m. having been transformed in sixty hours. I could see the light in their eyes dancing merrily as they embraced the many friends they had made in the past two weekends.

For me, this was a breakthrough evening. For me there was satisfaction that my sons had accepted another point of view for their lives that was different than their father's. My one fear had been that they would be badly influenced by his destructive qualities that basically amount to hating life, love, himself and others. What I wanted them to learn early in life was that there were other points of view in the universe besides that of their father.

Their glowing, radiant faces were a living testimony to me that they had learned their lessons well in the training, and that they, too, would reposition themselves in God's universe. Instead of cynicism and defensiveness I saw openness, awareness and joy. After the first weekend of the training I received a phone call at 3 a.m.

"Did we ever tell you how much we love you, mom?" came a voice booming over the phone. When I hung up, I went back to sleep with a profound sense of relief. Words like these are very rarely heard from teenage sons, but for me this heralded the beginning of the end of a long journey.

This wave of expansion and celebration spread like a virus through my family. The contagion of celebration is laden with joyous light from the love my sons have experienced since they took the Est training.

They radiate light—so much so that they have decided to convert the world. Penn Station and the Long Island Railroad are no longer safe for weary passengers who are about to get on the train. For my sons, the world is in need of total love and acceptance. I look out at the miracle of my new life and theirs.

My older son has just come back from climbing the Sierras and assisting at a new training that Werner Erhard created. He returned as if he had descended from the clouds. The music of the skies lit up his face. I could not believe the growth and expansion of his personality. While out West he had convinced his seventy-year-old grandmother and seventy-six-year-old grandfather that they, too, were in need of enlightenment.

So my mother, at seventy years, sat through two weekends on a stiff—backed chair to become enlightened. She sounded joyous when I spoke to her on the telephone. This contagion has spread so rapidly through the family that the West Coast contingent is covered! My brother took the training at the same time I did, but neither of us had discussed this with the other. A small miracle! When my father finishes his training, my aunt says, she, too, will join the family path to enlightenment.

Meanwhile I struggle through my days to find meaning for the future. I seek to hold the ways of the world in a context that allows for growth, joy, celebration and love. The entire scene of my life has changed in less than two years. My desire is to reach out and hug the stars, to run in the wind on a sandy beach. Today I sat in the sun and swam ten laps, noticing that I was able to be with myself in a way I couldn't in the past. How different the local swimming pool looked today from years ago when I sat encased in my marriage role, watching the waters anxiously as my sons dove from the high diving board. My mind travelled back to so many pools where I had to sit and watch the children splash and play. I was always filled with anxiety and never knew why I wanted to flee.

Now things have become clear. I was alone at the pool. I floated on top of the water looking up at the sunny blue sky fringed by tall evergreen trees. As I floated in the water, I felt the universe holding me up, buoying me with its power. I had only to relax in this bed of water and let the universe carry me upstream. There was nothing to do. It was all there. Joy, security, serenity and love were all there. I relaxed in the arms of the pool feeling the buoyancy of the waves surrounding me in the lazy, sunny afternoon.

Tomorrow I was to embark on a new step in my life, a new training, for my search was not over yet. I was still seeking that distant star, looking over the shoulder of heaven, for heaven knows what. But I knew now that my life was ready for miracles. I was raising the stakes.

For now, having been freed from the prison of my past, I decided that I wanted it all. Love, a visit to India with my guru, fame and fortune and I wanted everything right now. I was ready for the miracles of existence. I was open to the forces of tomorrow, ready and willing to embrace the future. I was ready to celebrate my freedom with joy and love. It was O.K. to live completely for I had earned my right to joy and life's rewards. Now I would step out onto the path of life and embrace all of it, just as simply as the waters of the pool had held me securely, floating and able to breathe the clear air and watch the sunlit blue sky.

So, too, could I float effortlessly toward the future, secure that God's love and miracles had indeed healed my wounded soul and now lit my path with sunlight. It was O.K. to reach out to all humanity, for we are one, and I clearly understood my connection to all there is on this earth.

Chapter 61

POINTS OF VIEW

Since I had breakfast at 7:30 a.m. this unexpectedly leaves me no choice but to write on my trip to Washington, D.C. I will try to express my experience of the here and now. These days, however, that is like trying to keep a whale inside a goldfish bowl.

Due to so many changes in my life I feel like I am back in college, staying up all night rapping about everything. Where do I want to go with my life and what do I want to do with it? This is, of course, a new phenomenon since I didn't have my own life before. I have just retrieved it from the major watershed of marriage and I find that I am totally unprepared to deal with having a life.

All of a sudden I am responsible for a life that belongs to me, not to my husband or my kids. That life was left behind. The thing that I waited and yearned for to happen for so many years finally happened. And I am in a panic. What would I do with myself when I got myself back was not a question I asked before. I was so busy running and running for so long just to get away from a bad marriage that I kept right on running past the place I should have stopped. Now, it's impossible to stop. I feel like I'm on greased roller skates going down a hill and ready to crash!

Having stayed up all night to see my sons graduate from the Est training, and having launched their transformed souls onto the Long Island railroad on the 5:20 a.m. train, I am now waiting in Blimpies (open all night) to get the 8:30 a.m. Metroliner to Washington, D.C.

where I hope to arrive in time to get some sleep before the scheduled cocktail party at the Hilton where I am staying for a conference of government-funded project directors.

At the moment, I am engaged in a really serious conversation with an Est trainer-to-be. We are discussing such anomalies as: "There is no table here, it's all in your mind."

"Sure, that's not a table, that's a collection of sluggish molecules. That's just an idea in your head! Of course there's a table, or I'd spill my cup of coffee on my lap."

At 5:45 a.m., over the third cup of coffee, waiting for the 8:30 a.m. Metroliner to Washington, D.C., I am trying to piece together all the fragments of my life still floating about in the cosmos. He and I are sharing our experiences of a seminar series called "The Body" that we are both taking and having become homework 'buddies', it is our task to discuss our respective body reactions and sensations that occurred during the past week.

I am just about to recover from the "About Sex Seminar Series" that I took jointly with another young man. That series challenged even more commonly-held assumptions than I had ever realized existed. Shock, hysteria and horror came up for me in that series. Considering the marriage I had endured, this didn't surprise me at all. When I entered the singles scene at forty sex loomed intensely as a monster from the deep which I have avoided dealing with in any rational way.

But early remarriage to avoid facing deeper issues about self, dependency, and the human condition seemed a worse alternative than being single and forty. Therefore, having embarked on the long-range search for self and inner peace all the issues that weren't clear were the ones that I wished to face and confront. As I stated earlier, my search has taken me through many disciplines and inner journeys. This search for completion and transformation brought me to Est. Since most people approach the Est training with reasonable attitudes, I can say I was different.

Having spent close to two years with a New-York-based ashram searching for inner peace, the Est training came as an explosion from my inner consciousness. One night at 4:00 a.m. I woke up from a dream hearing, "I have to take the Est training," in my head.

I looked around at the inky, dark night and fell back to sleep. The next day at work I received a phone call from Gena who was now working elsewhere since she had been fired.

"You have to take the Est training," she said. "I just finished it and you're coming as my guest to the post-training seminar."

"I know," I laughed. "I had a dream last night. I have to take the training."

"Then my phone call was no accident—you already have Est in your consciousness."

I agreed to go to the post-training seminar and signed up, still puzzled over the fact that I'd once heard Werner Erhard two years earlier and had thought, "Maybe, someday, I'll do this training." I had done other trainings and hadn't thought about Est until my dream the night before Gena's phone call.

Whatever divine calling led me to Est at 4 a.m. back then I'll never know. But here I was discussing my body at 5:50 a.m. with a young man hoping someday to become an Est trainer.

Life is an absolutely wondrous process. My experience of the path to peace had been a hilarious journey from beginning to end. Perhaps sorrow, terror and pain made it possible for me to appreciate the cosmic joke that's been played on mankind's little ego in the face of God's wider game board.

Now, as a graduate of Est, I have completed the sixty-hour training in repositioning myself in the universe in order to begin to accept satisfaction and the benefits of being human. I had come three-hundred-and-sixty degrees out of the 'dungeon of despond,' and I was beginning to come from an attitude of hope rather than hopelessness for I discovered many others in the world who shared with me one common ground, our humanity.

I have learned that I do not need to be ashamed of my past suffering and that, in the broad universe, my former husband represents only one point of view, which doesn't happen to be mine. Having escaped the confines of that point of view, I am seeking to trade my past sorrow for future joy. I have found my guru in India who speaks of life as a celebration and I am unlearning the 'doom and gloom' of the past for the joy of present laughter.

Now, I am not a person easily conditioned to joy, which comes hard for me. I am having to unlearn old patterns and tapes and allow trust and courage to be and to grow in my consciousness. It is like planting seeds in a newly tilled patch of earth It means tossing out negative head trips and accepting the world in the 'here and now.'

For me to accomplish this requires me to let go of a lot of fear. There seem to be deep, dark tunnels and caverns of fear within me which remain locked in my body and my consciousness. I know this may be the result of all the threats and abuse experienced in my marriage and I wonder often if I will ever trust again, or be able to create a relationship with a man in which I will not experience fear.

I hear Joseph saying, "You have to clean up that fear stuff with your ex—husband. You know that, don't you?" But my stomach gets into a knot and even though I nod my head, I run away from his words and introvert. Of course, what he is saying is correct, but it's always hard to get from here to there. I just know that I have much work to do on myself in order to root out mistakes and misconceptions in my mind that defeat me.

I live with a sense of expectancy and adventure about tomorrow. I am eager to find solutions to life's problems and I want to handle them as they come up. Life is an exciting process with many unknowns and a lot of surprises. I feel myself reaching upward and outward, expanding, floating, running, laughing and embracing life's potential.

This was, for me, one of the most complete surprises, because it was unexpected. I had expected my experiences would keep me down, hold me back and stop me. But the irrepressible power of the energy of life keeps bubbling up at me and saying "yes" to existence.

Chapter 62

TYPICAL BUSINESS TRIP

If my daily life at the office defies description, a typical business trip requires some pertinent details as well. Having now arrived at the distinctive stage of liberated lady executive working for a liberationist lady boss who believes all professionals must carry calling cards and attend professional conferences as often as possible, I am on my way to making my mark on the conference circuit.

This bestowed upon me the uncertain honor of winding up at numerous conferences and finding that most people sent on these trips were male. Looking around for a few female participants in all the strange and distant cities I was sent to visit, I did feel relieved to know that, although in the minority, some women did get to go on business trips, but not many, and not too often.

I have learned to enjoy hotels in strange cities, to talk knowledgeably on my subject and to realize generally that most women do not have the option of expanding their horizons in this way. Women are usually relegated to the clean—up squad, secretarial pool, office clerk or maid duty type of job. They serve their bosses and tend the hearth fires of our culture.

It's funny that when I leave on a business trip, Gerard is usually clucking around me like a mother hen, making sure I have my plane tickets (because he knows I'm absent minded), and seeing to it that all my papers are in my briefcase.

Before I leave home my freezer has to be full of food because my sons want to be certain they will not face famine in my absence. I also have to promise to bring souvenirs from whatever local ball team resides in the city I am visiting. There has to be enough cat sand, cat food and oil in the furnace before I leave.

By the time I have packed for the journey, my boss has usually tossed in one hundred and fifty pounds of books for me to display casually to every living thing en route, along with lists of the best restaurants within twenty-five miles of the vicinity I am about to visit.

There are days when I really don't want to leave because there is so much work to do at the office and there will be just that much more piled up when I get back. There are days when I have told her, "I don't want to go to California, I can't spare the time . . ."

"You'll work faster when you come back. It'll do you good to go to that conference in Disneyland. You look like you're dying from overwork—get some sun."

All of this, of course, is true. It's not just the conferences, but the pressure from my boss to finish my PhD at night. There are days when I dream fondly of going back to school and finishing—but there's no money. At least, not enough for my sons and myself to finish school. And to a good Jewish mother, who comes first?

One day she called me into her office to tell me: "You are always thinking of everyone else. You have to finish your education, too. After all, you want to move along in your career."

"I sure do—if it means more money."

"Well, after all, you're not getting any younger."

"Don't I know it."

"When are you going to finish your doctorate?"

"It's just that I have to plan for my sons' educations, then I can get back to myself."

"When will that be?"

"Soon . . ." In my head that looked like ten years, but I wasn't going to tell her that.

"OK. I'm going to keep after you."

The most touching thing was her kindness and concern. The insane thing is that I can't seem to find a way to get time or money for myself because all my existence has been channeled into others. My husband couldn't have planned it better. One of these days, I'll get even with him—and I'll get enough money to finish school, feed and educate my kids and even feed the cats, as well.

But when?

Chapter 63

ULCEROUS, EMPTY CHECKBOOK

I'm going to cop out pretty soon, just like my ex-husband did years ago. I'm tired of running this big, chicken-coop suburban house in Great Neck, the nesting grounds of Zelda and F. Scott. I'm tired of racing to keep the lights on, the telephone on and oil in the furnace. I am always a few days ahead of the nearest bill collector, and I feel like the ulcerated businessman, except I'm a woman so I earn a lot less for the same work. That, of course, doesn't sit too well with the bill collectors, so my stomach gets the brunt of it.

Every morning I stagger onto the LIRR, scene of thousands of male commuters escaping from their suburban wives and children. I join the peaked—looking morning crowd waiting anxiously to make the nearest broken-down New York City subway which will carry us luxuriously to work in funny, money city.

When I carry my briefcase onto the train each morning looking like Ms. Executive herself, I wonder what all these guy's wives are doing all day back in Great Neck or Washed Port or Mad Hasset. They slip into the great city each day, and slip back each night into the arms of suburbia. I slip in and out too, wondering what a freakish life I am living. I wonder why I'm not playing tennis in my miniskirt and buying expensive clothes that my husband can't afford to pay for. Instead I'm sitting on the train trying to balance my ulcerous, empty checkbook. There never seems to be enough money for the necessities.

Add to my crowning success my older son, a proud scholarship recipient at a fine, Ivy League college—and with that all the bills that add to my bankrupt bank account. When I figure out that I earn about fifty percent of what I'm really worth because I'm a woman, and that my ex-husband who turned himself into a basket case at thirty-nine has left me with two-hundred percent of the responsibilities, the addition and subtraction leave me dizzy, anxious and with a very acid stomach on the 7:09 train into the city.

I try to lull myself into a cheerful amnesiac state so that I will arrive at my office looking bright and affluent. All good jobs always go to affluent people. Therefore no one must know how you struggle to pay the grocer, the doctor or the drug store. For in our great society we always kick the loser.

The loser is that person who has been beaten down by the insane pressure to pay all the bill collectors, and who has stopped smiling. So I keep on smiling. My ex-husband, on the other hand, has given up. His Harvard diploma and advanced degrees from Brown, Columbia and NYU have all entitled him to the proud occupation of taxicab driver in New York City.

His inner self-image has been all but destroyed. Starting out as a Quiz Kid on national radio he now spends the greater part of each day contemplating suicide; he has decided to cop out. A weekly series of phone calls from him carries his usual message, "I can't take it anymore. I fail at everything I do. I want to kill myself—and my kids don't care about me. I have no sex life—and you don't love me."

Having heard this *ad nauseam* even when he earned $190,000 a year I have stopped listening. After close to twenty years of wedded bliss in which he has not moved a hair's breadth towards what Maslow calls self-potentiation I decided several years ago that he'd be better off without me.

But he wasn't.

So getting a legal separation from him was the closest thing to high-level negotiations ever encountered by man or beast. Having finally acquired this carefully-trussed document in my hot, little hands after four years of hair splitting, agonizing threats and repeated violence it is short of a miracle that I have maintained my sanity. And, I'm not absolutely certain that I have.

Trying to juggle two teenage sons on the brink of beating up their father for copping out on them just when they are on their way to college is not easy.

Neither is trying to keep the house from falling apart, since I can't afford repairs. And attempting to convince all these men to sell this huge, white elephant, because I am not the Ford Foundation or even Andrew Carnegie, has come to no avail.

So I swallow my anguish each day and join the ulcerated commuters from Mad Hasset and Great Neck and trudge into the city to find fame and fortune. The only way I survive these days is by reading Mary Baker Eddy. Since I can't pay doctor's bills—and I certainly can't afford a psychiatrist at $200 bucks a 50-minute hour—all that's left for me is to become a Christian Scientist.

Having been born a Chassidic Jew with my grandfather, whose namesake I am, a Talmudic scholar, I often wonder how I can unite these two, unfathomable faiths. Mysticism seems the only answer. Because, after all, I have to stay sane and I have just two choices. I can't remain Jewish because I have so little money to pay doctors—and most of the doctors I know in New York are Jewish.

If I get sick I'm really wiped out because I support my family, so I have become a health nut to survive. I read Mary Baker Eddy to save on doctor's bills—or else I should marry a Jewish doctor (I hope they don't charge their wives for medical care.)

The struggle to stay alive and beat the system is almost impossible. The only answer is FAITH.

Faith in anything. I've tried believing in everything—Eastern metaphysics, transcendental meditation, yoga, Zen Buddhism, bioenergetics, Gurdjieff, transactional analysis, existentialism, woman's lib, psychoanalysis, values clarification, Simon, Maslow, Rogers, Berne, May, Sartre, De Beauvoir, Kierkegaard, Friedan. But that doesn't pay my bills.

The whorish hand of the bill collector is always beating on my ulcerated stomach and the back of my head. Sometimes I can't sleep because I worry so much—but usually that works out pretty well because I use up a lot of calories not sleeping and it keeps my figure in shape.

I often indulge in wild flights of fantasy or day dreaming because I keep looking for a way out. My usual day dream consists of finding a millionaire (one who spends his money) to save me and my children from the wolf of destruction (famine).

Sometimes I indulge in the independence fantasy. I am going to be rich and famous. No man is going to support me and my sons. I am going to make it on my own. The world is going to find my genius in my little corner of Great Neck, and they will discover still another F. Scott, only female.

I listen to vibrations a lot when I am not adding up my check book and finding the usual balance of $3.03 till next Tuesday. This usually throws me into a panic and I stop eating. I usually tell my kids, it's time to stop buying food. They'll have to eat anything that is around the house until the next pay check. They've been pretty good about that, except I can't tell my younger son's five cats the same thing. They don't speak English. Fortunately cat food is cheaper, but when they go on austerity it means dry food for them. They let me know how little they enjoy eating dry food for five days at a time by throwing up on the living room carpet.

When my paycheck arrives we all eat again for about ten days, but it's the other four that usually leave me in a panic. When tuition is due at the great Ivy League college the whole world stops and I go into a suicidal panic. All relatives are called, the panic switches are pushed all over the country and I feel like a collection agency for some charity. My sense of dignity suffers in this crash program to pay the tuition for the semester. I spend about ninety percent of my days praying that my furnace won't run out of oil because I can't afford tuition and a full oil tank at the same time.

My third fantasy is to fill my house with itinerant writers, actors and artists who will all pay rent. I want to start a commune, but my kids scream they want privacy. They don't want strange people on their private property. Privacy is very costly!

And then there's my fourth and fifth fantasies.

My fourth fantasy is that one of my past loves will come back and rescue me from my menopausal demise having realized that he has loved me all these years. Of course, he will have achieved monumentally and, of course, he will love my children and help me to get them through their education.

My fifth fantasy is that my ex-husband will regain his self-respect and come back from the cop-out trip he's put himself on. And finally, the last fantasy comes when I collapse in despair. I am absolutely, totally helpless, sick and in desperate poverty, having failed to meet the creditor's demands—abandoned, old, alone and unloved. This fantasy takes me into the sad confines of desperation and grief and brings me to near-insanity until I call a friend to hear the magic words: "You're playing helpless again!"

Chapter 64

WOMEN ARE HISTORY

One day, Melinda, my boss, came to my office and asked if I could write a proposal for the Wonder Woman Foundation. I was surprised. "You mean, the comic book super heroine, Wonder Woman?" She replied affirmatively. "Just write a proposal of one or two pages, that's all they want."

That certainly was a simple request. Warner Communications and Maureen, the liaison from the Wonder Woman Foundation, had asked for a simple proposal from the youth agency. I dreamed up a series of multiethnic women's conferences, one for Asian American women, one for Black American women, one for Hispanic American women and one for Native American women. Warner Communications liked the idea and since they had just named their new foundation the Wonder Woman Foundation, the concept hit a nerve over there. D.C. Comics decided to develop a patch with Wonder Woman embroidered on it. It was beautiful in red, black and yellow embroidery. Such a special patch certainly needed a distinctive name. We had just been funded by and produced a series of conferences for Avon on diverse women and we had a lot of great women to call upon for our new conferences.

The Native American women who came represented a number of women tribal chiefs and several other women from around the United States from places such as Texas, Connecticut and Wisconsin. We invited Hispanic American women in leadership roles such as Aurora Mojica and Elba Cabrera, women from the Asian American community such as Sharon Hom, Esq. and women from the African American community such as Frankie Muse Freeman, Esq.

We named the badge *Women Are History*.

Chapter 65

POPE JOHN PAUL II

At my office, I had met with an Australian social worker who came to share with me the need for programs for delinquents in her country. I asked her about delinquency in Australia and she said it was indeed a problem.

At the time she said there had been a rash of fires in the forests near many towns in Australia and police were concerned that they had been set deliberately by teens looking to create mischief. This woman said, "Oh yes, the country needs preventive programs to work with youth." I gave her a pamphlet we had done on Juvenile Justice which perhaps had some programmatic ideas that might be worked on with Australian youth.

While we talked she mentioned "sex slavery" taking place in South East Asian nations where up country girls were sold by their parents to people who promised to educate them and give them jobs. Of course, that's not what happened to these girls and their lives were ruined when they were sold into prostitution once they were taken from their parents. For this loss of a young girl's life and future, the parents were paid enough to buy a television set.

She promised to keep me informed and on a master list related to these issues. From time to time there had been conferences on this alarming problem with attempts to rescue these underage girls and place them in orphanages where they were housed, fed and schooled. Many of them suffered severe trauma and needed a great deal of rehabilitation if they were ever to grow up and lead productive lives.

As we talked I felt anguish for these young, rural Southeast Asian girls. So many people wanted to rescue them and spare them the consequences of this terrible exploitation of the innocent. Many nonprofit organizations were getting involved and trying to put an end to these practices. I was happy to participate and help in any way that I could.

One day, out of the blue, I received an invitation from Pope John Paul II to an International Youth Conference at the Vatican. I was thunderstruck at the list of guests: Mother Theresa, Elie Wiesel, the chief Rabbi of Rome, the Rome Symphony Orchestra and on and on. What an honor to receive an invitation and to be invited to attend such a magnificent conference to discuss the problems of the world's youth.

Since my company would not be expected to send me I offered to go on my own dime, but first I extended my own invitation to the head of my community organization as a courtesy and sign of respect before availing myself of the honored visit to the Vatican. After having sent a memo upstairs to the powers in charge of the organization for which I worked, I asked for a response so that I night make plans to go to Italy and accept the invitation if they did not wish to attend. Many weeks went by and I never heard anything from upstairs. Finally I was told the invitation was sent to the International Office in London and they were told they could choose to accept or not.

Clearly my invitation had disappeared down the rabbit hole like Alice in Wonderland and I never got to attend and neither, as far as I know, did anyone from the International Office. What a sad way to treat a very honorable invitation. I am glad I am Polish like the Pope, even though I'm not Catholic. I would have liked to accept this invitation myself and go at my own expense. But it didn't happen!

Chapter 66

MY BROTHER'S WINERY

I would like to reconnect with my brother, with whom I maintain a civilized, if distant, relationship. He now lives in Oregon, owns a vineyard and makes wine. His wife is Chinese and his first daughter was born to a Mexican woman who worked for a Los Angeles family and wanted her baby to be adopted.

My brother and his wife Patty were delighted to take the baby home. She is named Rebecca and wants to be a professional athlete; I saw her last August.

My brother's second daughter was carried by an Indochinese surrogate; she is half his and half Indochinese. She is a whiz kid, incredible at schoolwork and over time she has wanted to be a dancer and a writer and now she is in her last year of high school. It will be interesting to see what her career choice turns out to be. Her name is Leah.

We live three thousand miles apart. Several years ago we went out to see him and his family in Oregon. By then my father had passed away and my mother was living with them. She wanted to go back to her home in California. My sons and I had visited them all many times. I loved Berkeley, California where they all lived.

After coming to Berkeley to finish his PhD my brother abandoned that career, took Est and became an entrepreneur. He ran for City Council and lost. But after thirty years he left, moved his family to Oregon and bought many acres of land. He planted grapes, renovated the house on the property to show wide picture—window vistas of the surrounding countryside, and then acquired some goats, a lot of pets (cats, dogs and fish) and planted a garden which yields fresh vegetables.

When I visited him several years ago, it basically was to say 'good-bye' to my mother who was ninety-five years old. I'm glad I did because she died a year ago at ninety-seven, and I wouldn't have seen her unless I went.

We traveled by train across America, stopping in Florida to see my older son and his family, then moving across through the sagebrush to California to visit my younger son who lives in Los Angeles. We then travelled north to visit my mother and brother, Patty and the girls at his mini-ranch. It's funny how much the town he and his family lived in in Oregon resembled a mini-Berkeley. It was filled with art galleries, wine cellars and a live Shakespeare theatre as well as a campus of the University of Oregon. He just moved from Berkeley to a mini-Berkeley in Oregon.

It was so similar, yet distinctly different. Organic veggies from the whole foods market, fresh salmon at its finest and coyotes howling at night near the room we stayed in, which was a very elegant apartment above the five-car garage that my brother had built for his guests. The bed we slept on, however, was like a rock. So for the next and last night we stayed, he and a staff member lugged a mattress upstairs for us. That helped a bit because we had to get up at 4 a.m. the next morning to catch a bus to Portland, which was a delightful city.

We got to spend some time at Powell's Bookstore, the largest bookstore in the country. What a treat!

Also, I'm very proud of my friend who is now a Poet Laureate of San Francisco, Janice Mirikitani. She's a magnificent poet and is married to the Minister who runs Glide Memorial Church in San Francisco. She had worked as a social worker there with street children. For years I helped her distribute the poetry written by these homeless children. The proceeds went back to help these children, some of whom were as young as five years old. Janice worked with these young people to give them hope and to turn them around and she did. Years later Will Smith made a movie about a homeless man and his son who were taken in by Reverend Cecil at Glide Memorial Church called *The Pursuit of Happyness*.

Chapter 67

JYOTI, AN INDIAN WOMAN DOCTOR

The train is crammed with people as I get pushed on. I am carrying my bags, trying to stand up in the crowd. Another winter storm to fight. The heavens rain snow drops, turning the earth's business into ice. Ice, rage turned into frozen froth and salty tasting foam. Icy, spidery fingertips turn the branches of the trees into razors that cut across the frozen blue sky. Driftwood landing on the beach, having floated in the icy seas, is now frozen into icicles lying on the sand.

I am fearful as I leave my apartment. I am looking for a space to rest. I must find some peace on this patch of earth I inhabit. So, on my trek towards peace, I slosh through a foot of snow, not really sure if I should even be going outside. The doctors did say that I am suffering from exhaustion. I should go easy on myself. But here I am trekking out in a severe snowstorm. Running, once again, towards peace. A contradiction in terms.

The train is packed with people trying to get home for the weekend. I am trying to get to the end of the line. Where am I going? What am I doing? Why? I've never been to the end of this train line before. In this blinding snow storm I have left Great Neck to go to the beach where my friends have invited me to come and rest for a few days. I am hoping to find peace far away at the beach house my friends have rented.

Standing up in the crowded train I feel about to faint. An Indian girl smiles at me and we begin to talk. Finally the hordes of men get off the train and we both get seats opposite each other. As we chat, she tells me her name is Jyoti, which means 'light' in Sanskrit. She tells me that she is a doctor. We exchange phone numbers. She invites me to come to India and visit her sisters or even her parents who live in Mombasa in Kenya. I have told her how much I have wanted to visit India and Kenya. I've thought about that for years. Many times I wanted to go to India. Many of my friends have gone to live in Poona and I had worked with students from Kenya and Mombasa and these were places I always wanted to see. After telling Jyoti my dreams about these places, she generously invited me to come and visit her family.

Maybe that would be better. Maybe getting into an airplane and flying halfway around the world a few times will be a calming influence. I could shave my head, I think, and wear an orange robe and stay in a temple and witness the mad throng of humanity passing by. Maybe that would be the cure for my inner angst?

Jyoti and I said 'good-bye,' promising to stay in touch. We had come to the end of the train line.

The windows of the train are frozen white. The platforms between the trains are inches thick with snow. I walk down the train platform with my bags looking for the taxi stand in the icy, frozen night. It was a long way to the stand in the snow. My toes are frozen and wet as I get into the cab, which I share with others. We drive through the snowy darkness letting people off at different beach houses.

When the taxi arrives at the house my friends have rented from a New York City newscaster who only uses the house in the summer, I see a light on in the living room. I don't know who is home yet. The door is open and after I knock, I walk in and drop my bags. I take off my soaking boots while sitting on a small wooden chair in the hallway.

A voice from upstairs calls. It's John and he tells me that my friend Bob will be home soon. Finally I feel the quiet and realize that I am away from the telephones and pressures of my office as well as the loneliness I feel in my apartment. Here, I am on vacation. The storm is blowing up at sea. John, Bob's friend, lost a boat and a car in the last storm and is looking for higher ground to leave his new car on. He isn't taking any chances this time.

I go into the kitchen to boil some water for a cup of tea. As I am running the water for tea, I hear a thumping on the porch. Since the door is always open, I look to see if it's Bob, but it's his friend Nick. "My cabin is out of gas," he says. "I'm looking for a haven in this storm." He keeps his coat on because the house is chilly. The windows of the front room look out to sea, and it is velvety blue outside with snowflakes gently falling.

I am suddenly aware of the quiet. There is a gentle peace that surrounds me inside the storm. I sit quietly sipping my tea. I am glad to be inside. I have come to be alone but with people near me. Alone to rest and to be with people nearby in order to escape my fear of aloneness. I have been running from a lonely terror, lately. Searching, running—hysteria pulling at my heart—and I ask myself when will it all end?

The night is dark and snow-filled. I have come to find completion. I wish to complete my personal mission. There is only a small distance to travel now. The storm takes on symbolic significance for me. I have faced the storms of my life untiringly and am willing to find the light to lead me into the future.

Jyoti's name flashes in my mind. It means light. In the darkness of the snow-filled night and surrounded by the sea and the snow-covered sand, I sit quietly, willing to be, and waiting for my friend Bob to return.

As the storm blows outside, I am sitting in a room on the sea side of the house filled with glass windows on all sides. In the dark outside the windows I can see the breath of the wind howling on the beach, whipping up white piles of snow. Flakes beat against the glass and form patterns on the windows in the night.

John is fearful this night. The last storm two weeks ago flooded the house, knocked out all the electricity, swept his car under the water and he hasn't recovered from the shock yet. "Even my boat sank," he said. "All these disasters entered my life after I met Sherrie. Maybe, now that our relationship is over, things will get better for me," he said hopefully. "I hope this is not a northeaster, but it might be," he said, looking very sad.

When Nick thumped on the door, John asked him to escort him to a place where he could leave his car on higher ground. They both left, pulling the door shut behind themselves. I sat there astounded to be in a place where no one ever locks their door. I sat very puzzled by this. There was actually a place where this happened. I, who have been running and hiding for so long, did not know or understand how such openness and trust could still exist. I thought that went out in the 1930s. There was so much fear inside me. I couldn't understand the existence of a place where people were still unafraid. My heart constantly quivers with fear and terror, always ready to stiffen with distrust if I feel panic setting in. I can't believe there is a way to live without fear. Then I heard Bob thumping up the stairs carrying three bags of groceries.

When he saw me he asked, "Did you have trouble getting out here?"

"Well, the train ride took two hours, but the five-mile taxi ride took another hour and a half. They took people to the furthest point first and then dropped me off at the end of the ride," I laughed as I told him about my saga in the storm.

Now I felt glad to be safe. We both put the groceries away.

Nick thumped in a few minutes later with John. I watched them all laughing and teasing each other. I was a little frightened since they were engaged in men's jokes. I tried to keep my center. It was true that I, being a woman, might be a drag.

I was reading *The Alpha and Omega,* a book on the treatises of Patanjali about witnessing our own consciousness. I tried to witness the scene. Time is always too short to capture all the experiences we need to remember.

Bob pulled out two chickens and John was elected to make the stuffing. But there was no stuffing.

"I've got some bread," said Bob.

"No way," said John. "Nick and I will go out to get some."

"Bring some wine when you come back," I said. "I don't drink hard liquor."

John looked at me.

"Is it too far away to get in this storm?" I asked.

He laughed, "No, no—we'll pick up some wine."

Bob and I were in the kitchen trying out his new toy, a microwave oven.

I was fearful and he reassured me that it was the worst model on the market with the most leakage.

"Why did you buy it?" I asked.

"Because it was the cheapest one."

"But the radiation could destroy your progeny," I said.

He laughed. "I'm not afraid of radio waves."

"What do they do?" I asked.

"They can burn holes in your body right clear to the bone," he said laughingly.

I didn't laugh and I didn't think that was terribly funny. But, then again, I'm not that well versed in modern technology and Bob, who was taking his master's in engineering, was. Of course, he was pulling my leg.

Nick and John thumped back up the wooden stairs carrying wine and stuffing and seasoning for the chickens. There were a lot of jokes about the stuffing—tasting, poking, laughing—and we also baked some potatoes and ate them with sour cream and scallion sauce.

John stayed in the kitchen crying over the onions he was cutting up for the stuffing. It was good and spicy. I decided to put hot sauce on the outside of the chickens to give them a little more zip.

We were all laughing and drinking wine, and I felt the tears running down my face because everything seemed so funny. Nobody was sure how long it really took to cook a microwave chicken and the search also began to find pans large enough to cook them.

Finally our festival began. The microwave memory was punched and the beeps kept coming at us every five or ten minutes. It was almost like being on a space ship. There was no way to leave in this storm, so Nick had to stay over because his cabin in the woods nearby was out of propane gas and was about to freeze.

There was a lot of laughing and a lot of fooling around as we waited for the chickens to be ready. Nobody was quite sure why the cook book didn't tell the truth about cooking time. John also wanted crisp skin, so he put the chickens in the conventional oven at the end.

John kept mooching cigarettes from me, even though they make him sick. I wish I could give up smoking, but currently, I can't. I remember laughing all night until the tears rolled down my cheeks. I don't remember what I was laughing about. The conversations during dinner covered the world, relationships between men and women, bad marriages, parents, rotting potatoes, refrigerated onions, the stock market, computer technology and their friend Will.

"You know that guy you met at the party last week?" said John.

"Yes—he seemed really nice."

"I have to tell you something about him."

"What?"

"He's married with a lot of children. Terrible marriage. Terrible. Never has anything to do with his wife. Hasn't in years."

I was surprised that Will had lied, but not really surprised that he was in a bad marriage.

"But he said he had never married," I laughed. "Why did he do that?"

"Because he figured you wouldn't really rap with him unless he said he was single."

"Oh, come on—I know about bad marriages. That's no excuse.".

It didn't really bug me because Will didn't interest me in that way, but if he did I would have been furious. "It would have been better if he'd told the truth," I said. It's always better when you come on straight. I could understand his unhappiness—but not the deceit. What's the point of that?"

John laughed.

"I guess people don't like to talk about their marriages in public," I thought. "They think they should hide them. Maybe in closets. After all, what's life all about anyway but bad marriages? Probably no one has seen a good one in so long they wouldn't recognize it. It might just pass them by and they wouldn't know it had anyway."

I kept picking up the book *The Alpha and Omega* every time there was a lull in the conversation because I was searching for something. I was trying to expand my 'witnessing consciousness.'

I was alone in a house in a storm with three guys because John's girl friend, who had been living there, left and they broke up their relationship for the fourteenth time. I was certain that outside the storm would subside. I was certain that I felt afraid inside myself. What was I doing here? I wondered if they thought it strange that I had come to their beach house to be alone and also to be with people. They didn't make much fuss about my femaleness and that was a relief. John was trying to get over his latest break-up. Bob and Nick were into equations from grad school and technical talk.

I found it easy to pick up the dirty dishes and put them in the dishwasher. That was a role I had always played, and since I hadn't cooked dinner, I felt kindly about helping to clean up.

I decided to go up the staircase to sleep because I had come for a rest and needed desperately to relax. I went into the little room where I was staying and lay down on the bed pulling the covers over me. I didn't take off the sweater I was wearing because it was still chilly, but my blue jeans were too tight to sleep in and I took them off and put them on a chair.

I kept trying to feel calm, but I was gripped with terror. I had come here to begin to finish my book—and it felt a dozen years away from completion. I couldn't get past the pain in my chest and I couldn't sleep.

After a while I kept thinking of Jyoti's name as I tried to calm myself. She said it meant, "Light." As I turned over in the dark, I tried to hold on to her name. "Light," I repeated. The laughter had stopped and Nick and John were watching late night television. Bob had fallen asleep in the chair, and then he pulled himself up the stairs and fell asleep instantly in his room. I felt very strange and worried that I might be in the way, unsure that I could find a place where I would really belong. I still felt like a wandering soul in the Ice Age. I was tossing and turning a lot, like the waves of the sea outside my window, and then, finally, I fell asleep.

The sunlight glared in through the window at six a.m. The storm was over. I went into the bathroom and took a bath. Everyone was still asleep. I pulled on my jeans and went downstairs. The sea was calm and the sunlight threw shadows across the orange curtains. I sat down in the living room with glass windows looking out at the Long Island Sound. I began sketching the chair, the plants in the room, the green and blue glass bottles on the window sill. I also read some parts of *The Alpha and*

Omega. I told myself that I was on vacation and I was supposed to rest. I was allowed to do whatever I felt like doing because those were the doctor's instructions. I was not to hassle myself.

It was hard for me to do that. I'd been so pressured and over-programmed in the past few months, it was hard for me to relax. Nick staggered out of the downstairs bedroom. It looked like he had slept in his coat and he was smiling. Bob came down the stairs ready to cook breakfast. John took his briefcase and went to work. Everyone was calm. The storm was over.

I welcomed a little space to be. And it was there.

Chapter 68

BATTERED WOMEN

This book was written because the incidence of battered wives and children has become a silent social scourge. The results of ineffective family relations between husband and wife in this country affect the lives of millions of children in many families. It is a highly electric topic with many 'hush hush' overtones. In the silent boudoirs of many American homes lurks a monster that has been swept under the rug, but that still remains to spread its tentacles through our entire society, thus reaching into the lives of many suffering people.

This book, *If I Had $1,500 I Would Clean My Karma*, is the story of a Harvard—and Columbia University-educated male with his college-educated Ivy League wife living in an upper class suburb surrounded by the affluence and the culture of the "well to do." The New York Times celebrated their wedding with an announcement. Yet years later, inside the suburban home in which they lived, there existed a barbaric feudalism that hardly warrants the twentieth century as a setting.

Perhaps this story is as old as time, but the struggle to overcome the barbarism and violence of a marriage which was life-threatening—while appearing to others as American as apple pie—should be a warning to all of us. Few women have had the courage to fight the battle for independence necessary to cut the umbilical cord of such a marriage, so these kinds of behaviors continue to flourish in many homes across the land.

The author of this book has told the story of her struggle to overcome constant threats against her life, almost on a daily basis. In the small details of her life and the love she felt for those around her was waged a ferocious battle to make life worth living and joyous. The struggle to transcend this barbarous marital relationship was also a struggle towards unity of self and the freedom for a true encounter with God.

Although some scenes read like the undertones of a Nazi prison camp, the basic theme of this book is the discovery that the victims in the battered wife syndrome must take action to deal with the reality they confront every day. Many women today are caught in this experience and feel helpless to fight their way to freedom. The author of this book hopes that the material contained in this manuscript will help to clarify this experience for many women who cannot articulate their feelings, but who suffer silently everywhere. These women do not represent a small number across the land. The most current available statistics say that there are between four and one half million to thirty million women in this country who may be considered 'battered.'

As a personal record of experience or a diary of events, this story will illuminate the eleven years of the author's life when she came upon the destruction of her final set of illusions and began a journey to recover her existence and her own freedom to be and to love. As she struggled to protect her children within a set of parameters that seemed insurmountable, she discovered her own strength and that of her children. It is time that we begin a conversation about these silent struggles within our culture. It is time to rip the mask off our behaviors and to examine our intentions, our own selves and our concept of family that has quietly ignored this terrible perversion of family life.

This story takes place in affluent suburbia with all the trappings we consider "the good life" still maintained on the surface. The increase of material wealth without a proper examination of the human values or ethics in male/ female relationships begets a dangerous lack of balance in all aspects of family life. The nature of this material can be considered terribly sad, even tragic, but the author has brought humor and joy and the warmth of human relationships to this story so each reader can feel a sense of empowerment and victory as they observe change taking place over insurmountable odds.

The author wishes this manuscript to teach us that if we fail to shed light on hidden family crime it will continue to grow in darkness. Unless we open the door to this subject and deal with it openly, rationally and positively, we will not be able to help the unfortunate women and children still caught in the vicious cycle of the 'battered' syndrome.

Many readers, both male and female, will be able to identify with this story because there is a thin line that separates all people from the anger that threatens to explode into violence. It requires strength, honesty and balanced judgment to maintain our integrity as human beings as we try to experience life with honesty in our pressure-cooker society.

A surprising aspect of this story of an upper-middle-class American woman is that she is hardly alone in her struggle. She represents a large cohort of American women who are still frightened into silence by their experience, and who may be unable to obtain police assistance. If they are finally able to achieve freedom they become a significant portion of escalating divorce statistics.

What adjustments are required by the individuals affected to help them believe that a trusting relationship with another person can ever happen again? Will our secrets remain buried or can the truth be told? These are questions that demand an answer.

For wives and children who are catapulted out of marriages such as these a strong support system will be required to help them readjust to life while leaving behind the bitterness, pain and horror they have experienced. Perhaps this book can help others who silently suffer and try to bury their terrors. Perhaps this book can show that family crime exists. It is my fervent wish that there be an end to this injustice and to the atrocities that people witness in their own homes.

If all the evidence of family crime were collected statistically, perhaps we would discover a mass of data that reveals an alarming picture of family life. As we look beneath the surface at the story of one woman's struggle to survive, we may gain insight into a severe social problem of our time that has not been fully viewed and that threatens families in epidemic proportions.

This story affirms life and while it presents the dark side it informs us that the restructuring of life must allow for the resurgence and belief in the value of people's self worth despite the trauma of beatings and violence. It is important to realize that understanding, humor and empathy at the poignancy of the human condition are paramount in healing those who have suffered these unfortunate events in their lives.

About the Author

This story documents a woman's life as she struggled to protect her children against insurmountable odds. Its location is in affluent suburbia with all the trappings of what we consider 'the good life'.

If we fail to shed light on this hidden family cruelty, it will continue to grow and unfortunate family members will be caught in this vicious cycle of 'the battered syndrome'.

This story took place before there were safe shelters and even laws against domestic violence.

As we look beneath the surface of one woman's struggle to survive, we may gain insight into a social problem that has yet to be fully addressed.

The author has written poetry, children's books, educational grants and materials for youth and adults.

Edwards Brothers Malloy
Thorofare, NJ USA
October 15, 2012